IT'S YOUR
Season

IT'S YOUR
Season

JERRY LEE WALKER III

LITTLE ROCK, ARKANSAS

It's Your Season
Copyright © 2020 Jerry Lee Walker III

All rights reserved, this book or any portion thereof may not be reproduced or used in any manner whatsoever without the express written permission of the publisher/author except for the use of brief quotations in a book review.

Printed in the United States of America

J. Kenkade Publishing
6104 Forbing Rd
Little Rock, AR 72209
www.jkenkadepublishing.com
Facebook.com/jkenkadepublishing

J. Kenkade Publishing is a registered trademark.

Printed in the United States of America
ISBN 978-1-944486-72-3

Table of Contents

Endorsements 7
Acknowledgements 11
Dedication 13
Needed Supplements 15
Introduction 17
Chapter 1: Experience the Goodness 27
Chapter 2: Agree with the Terms 39
Chapter 3: Inner Beauty 45
Chapter 4: Change of Attitude 71
Chapter 5: The Father's Identity 85
Chapter 6: God's Approval 101
Chapter 7: Supernatural Aptitude 107
Chapter 8: Put Your Gear On 117
Chapter 9: The Enemy's Profession 123
Chapter 10: The Setup 137
Chapter 11: Abundant Living 143
Chapter 12: Say So for Yourself 167
Glossary 181
About the Author 185
About J. Kenkade Publishing 187

Endorsements

Endorsement #1

Ambassador Walker's ability to share Biblical life principles in a practical and insightful manner is a refreshing addition to todays Kingdom writing. The prayer lives and Bible study of new Christian converts and seasoned believers alike will benefit from these teachings.

Ms. Rasheeda Hamilton
Academic Advisor/College Prep Consultant
MA Sociology

Endorsement #2

I feel blessed just to know Jerry Lee Walker III. Not only do I see Jerry talk about his faith and his God, but I get a chance to witness it firsthand through his action. I get to witness a devoted husband and father who loves God and who loves God's people. I'm inspired every time I read his social media posts, see something he's accomplished or see him interact with his family.

Monte Hodges
American Politician/Arkansas State Representative
BBA Business Administration

Endorsement #3

All of God's children are created in His image to live out their true purposes and highest callings in Christ. When I first met Jerry, I saw a Man with the favor of God upon him. By having the opportunity to work with Jerry in Kingdom assignments in the community, I have watched him become a man of his word, a Man of integrity, righteousness, deity and honor. Ambassador Walker strives daily to be the kind of Man our society needs today.

Rev. James E. Hollywood
President
Hollywood Business Services & Consulting, LLC
Public Administration Masters

I know in my heart that man is good. That what is right will eventually triumph. And there is purpose and worth to each and every life.

– Ronald Reagan

Acknowledgments

My gratitude to my family: Toni Walker (wife) Derreon (eldest son) India (daughter) Solomon (youngest son) who have shared me with this manuscript for months.

To my parents Jerry & Wendy, thank you for all that you've done for me. I feel as though you both have given me your all and I appreciate it. It's because of you two that the world gets me.

Thank you to Varonda Williams, who has supported my ministry through intercession, words of encouragement and just having an ear to hear.

I appreciate all of you very much.

Dedication

I dedicate this book to all the individuals who have dreams, aspirations and a desire to live a life of greatness. To those who are searching for more than what God can do for them but rather what God can do through them. This book is for them. People that realize they have a say so in how their life will turn out and how history will be made. It is my heart's deepest desire to see these individuals break away from the clutter of the common and realize their voice and authority. To begin to manifest their true and authentic selves without fear and care of the cultures and opinions that try to minimize their greatness. It is my belief that this moment, this very moment that you are in now reading this was predestined by God, so to you I say: this book is dedicated to you.

It truly is your season. You shall not be held back, tolerated, cheated of your inheritance or prevented from advancements or promotions any longer.

It's your season for things to come together. Your family, marriage, business, ministry, money, plans are all coming together!

Your season is here!

Needed Supplements

Make sure you have the right tools!

You will need:
- Bible- To turn to reference scriptures. God may bring further things to your remembrance, allow the Holy Spirit to guide you.
- Preparing for Harvest Devotional Journal, a pen and highlighter- This will assist with your daily devotions and help you to organize your thoughts and answers to questions that are in various chapters of the book and allows you to pull out things that really hit or register with your spirit.
- It's Your Season audio CD collection- A series of teachings that will bring more light to the messages in this manual. You will be able to play it in the car, while you're cooking, exercising, meditating before bed. It's an easy way to keep your focus on your season. IT IS HERE!

Introduction

Do you find yourself asking the question, "Is there more to life than the seemingly never-ending struggle of survival?"

Does life seem like a mystery?

Is it hard to see how the bible relates to today's times?

Do you believe that there is more to your life than the cycle of mediocrity and obscurity?

I'm here to let you know, THERE IS MORE! Through small daily, conscience decisions, you can live a life of MORE!

That more is your life in The Kingdom of God, your unlimited potential: "dormant ability, reserved power, untapped strength, unused success, hidden talents, and capability" is released through the knowledge of the Kingdom and of its Lord.

You can experience divine success and prosperity through aligning yourself with the Word of God.

There is more to you than what meets the eye. You are fearfully and marvelously made (Psalm 139:14). You don't have to go through life mediocrely. You can live a life of luxury, excitement and influence. You must tap into your treasure that's on the inside of you (2

Corinthians 4:7). Your heavenly father has provided for you all things pertaining to life (2 Peter 1:3).

You can live life abundantly through the Kingdom. The Kingdom of God gives you an advantage over the evil one, over worldly systems and over generational hinderances.

To access this divine inheritance, you must not live through your fallen human nature. The fallen human nature has character flaws that will halt the life that God promises to give you as an inheritance. Our fallen human nature is full of selfishness, divisions, evil cravings and impure practices and behaviors that will keep us from living that life of freedom.

When I talk about freedom, I'm not speaking from a carnal place, but I speak from the context of the Kingdom. Freedom is no longer being bound to the works of darkness, meaning ignorance.

I have created this resource, "It's Your Season," as a companion to the devotional journal "Preparing for Harvest" to show you the rewards you have if you diligently seek the father (Hebrews 11:6). You are a recipient of benefits that Christ died for you to receive (1 Peter 3:18). By following proper protocol and obeying Kingdom laws you can live the good life.

The good life is released through keys, that's what this book is, a key of a set of keys for you to break out of the "prison of the mind".

A man sooner or later discovers that he is the master gardener of his soul, the director of his life. – James Allen

Take the wheel of your life and begin to experience the success and prosperity that comes from following the directions that have been placed in the Word of God. The Word of God is not a book of "thou shall nots" but a book of "thou shall haves" and if you continue in it, success and prosperity is the inevitable.

As we will discuss in a later chapter your mind creates your life. The Word of God opens us up to the mind of God, his thoughts. Therefore, allowing his thoughts to become our thoughts will attract only those things which are of God. Good success and prosperity are of God!

This book of the law shall not depart out of thy mouth; but thou shalt meditate therein day and night, that thou mayest observe to do according to all that is written therein: for then thou shalt make thy way prosperous, and then thou shalt have good success.

Joshua 1:8

The Word of God has the power to realign our lives to the path of success and prosperity. Mindsets, belief systems, ideologies, traditions and doctrines all must be filtered by the Word of God.

Like a filter's job in the natural is to remove impurities, likewise is the job of God's Word. God's Word moves the impurities that we have been operating with, causing us to live a life that is less than God's best.

For I know the thoughts that I have towards you, says the Lord, thoughts of peace and not of evil, to give you a future and a hope.

Jeremiah 29:11

For your life to align with the above scripture, you must get your mindset, belief systems, ideologies, traditions and doctrines filtered through the Word of God. This is the only way that peace, goodness, hope and a future of maximizing your potential and fulfilling purpose will come.

Tap into the best version of yourself, the genius on the inside, your uniqueness and the you that God sees you as. Your only limiting factor is ignorance! Through the incorruptible seed of the Word of God (1 Peter 1:23) you gain victory over ignorance for the Word of God illuminates, gives knowledge and wisdom to matters.

When you stop reaching, seeking, looking, dreaming, you will see your life at a standstill, vulnerable for attacks of the enemy such as frustration, loneness, depression, jealousy and insecurity.

The precepts in this book will increase you, it's for your edification, your building up and for your advancement. I will take you to scriptures and site verses that reveal revelation that will give clarity to things that you hear about but really haven't gotten a context on it so that you understand the effect they have on your day to day life.

I'm a firm believer that if your context is wrong, then your conclusion is wrong, and if you have the wrong conclusion, your thought process and behavior will lead you down the wrong path. (Proverbs 14:12)

It is my intention to challenge your thinking that the Kingdom of God comes forth out of you. The time has come to an end, where you look outwardly for what has been in your possession all along (Luke 17:21).

Before going any farther, let's look at your identity. It's important that we do this now, so that you will have a clearer understanding of who you are and why the messages in this book is relevant to you.

Your identity must not be based on your job, career, relationship status, family roles or community roles or any external based thing. It should be founded on Kingdom truths. Kingdom truth will never fail, you will never get abandoned from them, fired, kicked out or neglected. This is the type of foundation you need your identity built upon for you to thrive and live an abundant life. The enemy wants you to believe you are your history. He operates by deceiving people to believing they are their past failures and mistakes keeping them from fulfilling their purpose, because if you don't know who you are you don't know what to do. You must have an assurance about who you are.

The value of identity, of course, is that so often with it comes purpose.
– Richard R. Grant

Kingdom Identity truths

You are a child of God
   Romans 8:16
   The spirit itself beareth witness with our spirit, that we are the children of God.

You are a new creation
   2 Corinthians 5:17
   Therefore if any man be in Christ, he is a new creature: old things have passed away; behold, all things are become new.

You are an overcomer
   1 John 5:4
   For whatsoever is born of God overcometh the world: and this is the victory that overcometh the world, even our faith.

You are blessed
   Ephesians 1:3
   Blessed be the God and father our Lord Jesus Christ, who hath blessed us with all spiritual blessings in heavenly places in Christ.

You are chosen
   1 Peter 2:9
   But ye are a chosen generation, a royal priesthood,

am holy nation, a peculiar people; that ye should shew forth praises of him who hath called you out of darkness into his marvelous light;

You are complete
Colossians 2:10
And you are complete in him, which is the head of all principality and power.

You are forgiven
Ephesians 1:7
In whom we have redemption through his blood, the forgiveness of sins, according to the riches of his grace;

You are loved
Jeremiah 31:3
The Lord hath appeared of old unto me, saying, yea, I have loved thee with an everlasting love: therefore with lovekindness have I drawn thee.

You are valuable
Luke 12:7
But even the very hairs of your head are all numbered. Fear not therefore: ye are of more value than many sparrows.

You are victorious
1 Corinthians 15:57
But thanks be to God, which giveth us the victory

through our Lord Jesus Christ.

You are no longer a slave to fear
   Romans 8:15

   For ye have not received the spirit of bondage again to fear; but ye have received the spirit of adoption, whereby we cry, Abba, father.

You are not a slave to sin
   Romans 6:5-7

   For if we have been planted together in the likeness of his death, we shall be also in the likeness of his resurrection: Knowing this, that our old man is crucified with him, that the body of sin might be destroyed, that henceforth we should not serve sin. For he that is dead is freed from sin.

You are the temple of the living God
   2 Corinthians 6:16

   And what agreement hath the temple of God with idols? For ye are the temple of God; as God hath said, I will dwell in them, and walk in them; and I will be their God, and they shall be my people.

   Congratulations! You've just been introduced to who you really are apart from being conformed to this world (Romans 12:2). In order to complete this new way of thinking and operating, you must continue in the Word of God for total transformation (Romans 12:2). If you have not already, you should grab "preparing for harvest devotional journal" to assist with your daily meditations. You will find in this book that not all scriptures are quoted but I have sited the verse. I want you to engage in a study with this resource, use it as a part of your daily devotions.

Let's get started on entering behind the veil of God's Glory and becoming more intimate with him as a father, being empowered through your union with him (Ephesians 6:10) causing you to impact your family, marketplace, church, community and nation in a remarkable way. You are a gift to humanity.

Winning is downloaded in your DNA.

Case and point: Before one sperm can reach the egg of a woman in the "race for life" it must compete with about 199 million other sperms, during this process the sperms go through a path of obstacles. They must go through tubes and avoid walls and avoid cells that will take them out of the game. During this process to the egg all sperms are trying to win. You were that winning sperm. You came into this world a winner. As a matter of fact, God himself predestined for you to win the race.

> Here is what he said:
> I chose you before I formed you in the womb;
> I set you apart before you were born.
> I appointed you a prophet to the nations.
> *Jeremiah 1:5*

Opening prayer

Father, speak to me and show me the way in which I should take, enlighten me that I may walk in revelation knowledge and be apart of releasing your Glory in all the earth. I desire to be like your dear son Jesus Christ therefore I study your Word and deliberately apply your commands to my life as a good son. Thank you, father, for every gift, talent, capability and strength you've given me, I know that by being in your Word you will perfect all of them because they concern me and as I cast my worries and anxieties to you, you're perfecting those as well, causing them to look like your original intent for my life, all things are working together for my good. I will not be drowned with sorrow, sadness, depression or debt. MY LIFE IS CHARACTERIZED BY LIBERTY!

In Jesus name,
Amen.

Chapter 1

✝

EXPERIENCE THE GOODNESS

It was for this freedom that Christ set us free [completely liberating us]; therefore, keep standing firm and do not be subject again to a yoke of slavery.
Galatians 5:1 (AMP)

There is an upgraded version of yourself, a version of you that you have yet to discover and the world is waiting on its debut (Romans 8:18). You have some-thing to offer, that no one else can. It's time for you to get in the game, put in the work of becoming the best you possible for this is the reason Christ made you free. That you may become everything that the heavenly father predestined you to be (Ephesians 2:10).

The only way one can truly began to release their potential as stated in the introduction their "dormant ability, reserved power, untapped strength, unused success, hidden talents, and capped capability" is to conqueror their fallen human nature by the works of the Holy Spirit. If we operate from the fallen human nature we will continue to live in a place of fear, doubt, worry, confusion and care. The fallen human nature is a place of limitations. It's a place of calculation and it's a place that will stagnate you from moving forward in life. If you become limited, and stagnated then the world cannot evolve into the place desired by God because there are certain things that only you can do.

It is you that can only fulfill your God given assignment! Others may have similar assignments, but no one can complete your assignment with accuracy, authenticity and clarity like you.

In your fulfilling of your assignment you bring solutions to problems, missing pieces to puzzles and answers to prayers.

Yes, God wants to use you to answer someone's prayer! They will say things like: "You're a life saver! What would we do without you? How did we ever make it without you?"

And he has given you a destiny- something to do in this life, something only you can do. Before you were born, God wired you with certain ambitions, desires, and drives to play a particular role in history- one that only you can play.
                                                        -Rick Warren

You must steward this earthen treasure well (2 Corinthians 4:7), that God may get a return on his investment. The treasure is your unlimited potential (Ecclesiastes 3:11) and God's return is having humanity pushed forward and his name becoming great in all the earth because of the glory that's on your life (Matthew 5:16).

But I say, walk habitually in the [Holy] Spirit [seek Him and be responsive to His guidance], and then you will certainly not carry out the desire of the [a]sinful nature [which responds impulsively without regard for God and His precepts].
Galatians 5:16 (AMP)

Sin is missing the mark from God's original intent for your life. It is God's original intent for you to live abundantly (John 10:10), prosperous and healthy (3 John 1:2) in peace (Psalm 29:11) and success (Isaiah 1:19). To not become better, bigger, brighter and display your brilliance is sin.

There is no passion to be found playing small- in settling for a life that is less than the one you are capable of living.
-Nelson Mandela

In order to live this life of releasing potential you must welcome the presence of God into your life, your body allowing him to dwell within you.

Therefore I urge you, brothers and sisters, by the mercies of God, to present your bodies [dedicating all of yourselves, set apart] as a living sacrifice, holy and well-pleasing to God, which is your rational (logical, intelligent) act of worship.
Romans 12:1 (AMP)

So here's what I want you to do, God helping you: Take your everyday, ordinary life— your sleeping, eating, going to work, and walking-around life— and place it before God as an offering. Embracing what God does for you is the best thing you can do for him. Don't become so well-adjusted to your culture that you fit into it without even thinking. Instead, fix your attention on God. You'll be changed from the inside out. Readily recognize what he wants from you, and quickly respond to it. Unlike the culture around you, always dragging you down to its level of immaturity, God brings the best out of you, develops well-formed maturity in you.
Romans 12:1-2 (MSG)

God is interested in our entire life. He wants to be involved in every aspect of it. He wants to help us take our ordinary life and make it a masterpiece.

When we willingly present God a body, our life and continue to allow him to have final authority- being obedient to his precepts his very presence produces fruit through us. This fruit is your divine nature. The bible says that if we will be willing and obedient, we will eat the good of the land (Isaiah 1:19). Are you ready to eat the good of the land? I'm here to let you know that you can get in on the good life.

The earth is the LORD'S, and the fulness thereof; the world, and they that dwell therein.

Psalm 24:1

It all belongs to our father and we are heirs of it (Romans 8:17), don't limit yourself by thinking you don't have the money, resources, connections or education to live a good life. If you will be willing and obedient you will eat the good of the land.

This is the reason you have been made free, so that you will live a good life, eat the good of the land. All the necessarily elements have been provided through the holy spirt for you to experience this good life.

Say this out loud:
"I'm going to make the rest of my life, the best of my life because the Word of God indicates I can."

The good life was preordained by God. Above we discussed that God's intentions for us are to live a good life, now we will explore deeper in text to clarify this statement.

For we are His workmanship [His own master work, a work of art], created in Christ Jesus [reborn from above— spiritually transformed, renewed, ready to be used] for good works, which God prepared [for us] beforehand [taking paths which He set], so that we would walk in them [living the good life which He prearranged and made ready for us].

Ephesians 2:10 (AMP)

For I know the plans I have for you," declares the LORD, "plans to prosper you and not to harm you, plans to give you hope and a future.

Jeremiah 29:11 (NIV)

We can sense the love and desire that God has for us to live a good life in these prophetic scriptures. The following points can be pulled from the above texts:
- You are a masterpiece created for good
- God has already planned your life from the beginning
- God's plan will bring prosperity
- God's plan will not harm you in any way
- God's plan has hope, despite your current circumstances
- God's plan always includes a future
- God has intentional plans for you

The good life demonstrated through Job:
The LORD restored the fortunes of Job when he prayed for his friends, and the LORD gave Job twice as much as he had before.

Job 42:10

The Lord blessed Job with twice as much as he had, which was equivalent to be multimillions because Job already walked in a great deal of wealth prior to the double portion.

And the LORD blessed the latter days of Job more than his beginning; for he had 14,000 sheep, 6,000 camels, 1,000 yoke of oxen, and 1,000 female donkeys.

Job 42:12

These animals in today's market would be about $40 million dollars. Why would Job need these animals? Did he have a transporting business hauling cargo and goods to the various cities and trading posts? This would indicate that God's goodness was shown in Job's business as well.

After this, Job lived 140 years, and saw his sons and his grandsons, four generations.

Job 42:16

This was the good life demonstrated through Job:
- Increase in cash flow
- Material wealth and blessings
- Increase business operation/production
- Long life
- Generational sustainment

The wisdom to obey God's instructions leads to a good life.

[The wisdom from above] are there any of you who are wise and understanding? You are to prove it by good life, by your good deeds performed with humility and wisdom.

James 3:13 (GNT)

We prove that we are wise and have understanding by living the good life and doing good to others. God doesn't get any glory out of our mediocrity, obscurity or foolish and perverse behavior. Wisdom is an important key in living the good life.

Wisdom gives: a long, good life, riches, honor, pleasure, peace.

Proverbs 3:16-17 (The Living Bible)

Grow a wise heart- you'll do yourself a favor; keep a clear head-you'll find a good life.

Proverbs 19:8 (MSG)

A clear head has two parts, meaning to have:
- Understanding
- Focus

Knowledge is knowing and wisdom is the application of knowledge to help you succeed. God wants his people to walk in knowledge and wisdom.

If any of you lacks wisdom [to guide him through a decision or circumstance], he is to ask of [our be-

nevolent] God, who gives to everyone generously and without rebuke or blame, and it will be given to him.
James 1:5

Wisdom will lead to obedience to the Word of God.

My father taught me this: pay attention to what I say. Obey my commands and you will have a good life.
Proverbs 4:4

If you obey the commandments, you will have a long good life in the land the Lord promised to your ancestors and to you, their descendants- a wonderful land flowing with milk and honey!
Deuteronomy 11:9 (The Living Bible)

My son listen to me and do as I say, and you will have a long, good life.
Proverbs 4:10 (The Living Bible)

God's Word is full of instructions that will allow us to experience life more abundantly.

Life's tragedy is that we get old too soon and wise too late.
— Benjamin Franklin

Honor & integrity lead to a good life

Honor God
Wherefore the LORD God of Israel saith, I said indeed that thy house, and the house of thy father, should walk before me forever: but now the LORD saith, Be it far from me; for them that honor me I will honor, and they that despise me shall be lightly esteemed.
1 Samuel 2:30

Honor the LORD with thy substance, and with the first fruits of all thine increase.
Proverbs 3:9

Honor your Parents
Honour thy father and mother; which is the first commandment with promise; That it may be well with thee, and thou mayest live long on the earth.
Ephesians 6:2-3

Honor your Spouse
Likewise, ye husbands, dwell with them according to knowledge, giving hon-our unto the wife, as unto the weaker vessel, and as being heirs together of the grace of life; that your prayers be not hindered.
1 Peter 3:7

However, each man among you [without exception] is to love his wife as his very own self [with behavior worthy of respect and esteem, always seeking the best for her with an attitude of lovingkindness], and the wife [must see to it] that she respects and delights in her husband [that she notices him and prefers him and treats him with loving concern, treasuring him, honoring him, and holding him dear].

Ephesians 5:33

Honor your Elders

Show respect to the aged; honor the presence of an elder; fear your God. I am GOD.

Leviticus 19:32

Honor your Boss

Servants, be submissive to your masters with all [proper] respect, not only to those who are good and kind, but also to those who are unreasonable.

1 Peter 2:18

Honor your Church Leaders

Now we ask you, brothers and sisters, to appreciate those who diligently work among you [recognize, acknowledge, and respect your leaders], who are in charge over you in the Lord and who give you instruction, 13 and [we ask that you appreciate them and] hold them in the highest esteem in love because of their work [on your behalf]. Live in peace with one another.

1 Thessalonians 5:12-13 (AMP)

Honor Governmental Officials

Let every person be subject to the governing authorities. For there is no authority except from God [granted by His permission and sanction], and those which exist have been put in place by God. Therefore whoever resists [governmental] authority resists the ordinance of God. And those who have resisted it will bring judgment (civil penalty) on themselves.

Romans 13:1-2

Living the good life takes knowing God's Word and having the discipline to implement what it says in your day to day life.

Chapter 2

Agree with the Terms

Can two walk together, except they be agreed? -Amos 3:3

God will never walk with us as we fulfill the lusts and the desires of the flesh. He's not a God that's in agreement with sin. Everything God does is integral; he will not do anything outside of his nature! We can look throughout the bible and prove that God is a God of increase, promotion, advancement, and championship status.

God is a God that changeth not (Malachi 3:6), he'll never leave us or forsake us (Hebrews 13:5). We decide to leave and forsake him when we began to operate in our sinful fallen human nature. Fashioning ourselves after fear, worry, doubt, and care. The wonderful thing is that God will be right where we left off, so never feel that it's too late. Repent, that is change your thinking and get back on the winning team.

If we live by the [Holy] Spirit, let us also walk by the Spirit. If by the Holy Spirit [we have our life in God, let us go forward walking in line, our conduct controlled by the Spirit.]

Galatians 5:25

There are distinctions of fruit between those who walk according to the evil human nature and those who walk according to the Spirit. Matthew 7:16 records that you will know people by the fruit they bring forth.

We are to be the FBI (Fruit Bearing Inspectors). We can discern and know whether people and especially ourselves are under subjection of the evil human nature or God's nature. Live under God's nature, happen to life don't allow life to happen to you, you have a say so in how your days and years will be spent (Job 36:11).

Jesus promised that the Spirit would be a source of help for us to ensure we bear good fruit.

And I will ask the Father, and He will give you another Comforter (Counselor, Helper, Intercessor, Advocate, Strengthener, and Standby), that He may remain with you forever. The Spirit of Truth, Whom the world cannot receive (welcome, take to its heart), because it does not see Him or know and recognize Him. But you know and recognize Him, for He lives with you [constantly] and will be in you.

John 14:16-18

He also promised that the Holy Spirit's power would help his followers to spread the gospel around the world. World meaning systems.

The Gospel of the Kingdom should be carried throughout the following systems:
- Educational
- Political
- Medical
- Media
- ALL INDUSTRIES

You shall receive power (ability, efficiency, and might) when the Holy Spirit has come upon you, and you shall be My witnesses in Jerusalem and all Judea and Samaria and to the ends (the very bounds) of the earth.

Acts 1:8

We must follow in the straight and narrow path to a life of freedom that Jesus has trailblazed for us to walk and live in, not bound by ignorance.

> Because strait is the gate, and narrow is the way, which leadeth unto life, and few there be that find it.
>
> *Matthew 7:14 (KJV)*

> All who declare that Jesus is the Son of God have God living in them, and they live in God
>
> *1 John 4:15*

This truth, no other religion or philosophy can claim. No other has implied the living presence of its god or lord in his followers. Muhammad does not live in Muslims. Buddha does not inhabit Buddhists. Hugh Heffner does not inhabit the hedonist.

They all may offer influence, instructions, enticement, yes, but the power or ability to occupy those that believe, no.

As Christians we belong to Jesus Christ. Even more in depth, we are becoming him more and more. Conforming to his image.

Christ moves into us and makes adjustments to our way of living. He gives new purpose to bad decisions, and by Spending time with him allows us to see our new image emerging.

> For whom he did foreknow, he also did predestinate to be conformed to the image of his Son, that he might be the firstborn among many brethren.
>
> *Romans 8:29 (KJV)*

Allowing the Spirit to be a part of your daily activities is as easy as A-B-C.

A- Admit. Admit that your way of doing life has been wrong, you have misaligned life strategies.

B- Believe. Believe that the Word of God is the answer to success, prosperity and happiness.

C- Commit. Commit your ways to the Word of God. Speak your commitment privately and publicly. Actively demonstrate your commitment through your lifestyle.

Out of all the things we have to earn in life, a relationship with God is not one of them. We must simply Admit, Believe and Commit. God, the father is available to transform us from the inside out. He is always speaking to us and always wanting our attention. He waits for the day of our transformation into his dear son (Romans 8:29) through engaging in daily fellowship with him.

Agree with the terms of Admitting, Believing, Committing.

It's not enough that we do our best; sometimes we have to do what's required.
— Winston Churchill

Chapter 3

Inner Beauty

It is God's will to brand us, making us stand out from others and making us royalty (1 Peter 2:9). The fruit of the Spirit is our brand. It's what says that you are a man or woman of God. This branding is not a branding on the external where people can see a label on your body but it's a branding of your internal that results in the exterior being impacted for the better. People can see it through your choices and decisions of producing a healthy lifestyle.

So much emphasis is put on our outward appearance: how we look, what we drive, where we live and we could continue on, but it's what's on the inside that really matters and that's what my focus is to help you develop. Outer beauty is vanity, but inner beauty is pleasing to the father. It's the inner beauty that's full of character, integrity, morals, values and standards.

When the enemy shall come in like a flood, the Spirit of the LORD shall lift a standard against him.
Isaiah 59:19

Your internal being is the standard in which God is raising up!

Inner beauty will keep you grounded, stable, secure in times of trials and tribulation (John 16:33). It's through inner beauty that Jesus was able to live effectively on earth, so it's by inner beauty you and I shall live effectively on earth.

All goals will require you to have inner beauty in order to achieve them.

Areas in which you should have goals in include:
- Personal
- Spiritual
- Relational
- Financial
- Professional
- Vocational or Industry Specific (your work)

This inner beauty that I am speaking of is the fruit of the Spirit. This is the reason God looks at your heart and not your outward appearance! (1 Samuel 16:7).

Your gifts, talents, abilities and all the things you do well may get you exalted but it's your character, your inner beauty that will keep you there (Proverbs 18:16). You'll be influential, leaving a legacy, making history, shaping humanity and establishing God's Kingdom here on earth.

The most important human endeavor is the striving for morality in our action. Our inner balances and even our very existence depend on it. Only morality in our actions give beauty and dignity to life.
– Albert Einstein

The integrity and moral courage of the upright will guide them, but the crookedness of the treacherous will destroy them.

Proverbs 11:3

Divine Character

I've included a prayer after each divine characteristic, you should use the power of your voice and words and pray them aloud with authority.

But the fruit of the Spirit is love, joy, peace, patience, kindness, goodness, faithfulness, gentleness, self-control. Against such things there is no law.
Galatians 5:22-23

Love
Love sees and operates as God sees and operates.

For God so loved the world, that he gave his only begotten Son, that whosoever believeth in him should not perish, but have everlasting life.
John 3:16

Notice the first few words of the above scripture "God so loved the world, that he gave." What we can find out here is that we should have a love for humanity enough to give to its evolution. To enhance it make it better. This is what Thomas Edison did with electricity and the wright brothers with the airplane. They helped push humanity further because of a love they had. They carried a seed of solution, missing pieces to a puzzle and were the answer to someone's prayer.

They tapped into their earthen treasure, releasing potential that had never been discovered before and it changed the way humanity operates on a daily basis.

Do you love the world enough, the next generation, your unborn children, grandchildren, to do your part in shaping this world? What creative idea do you have or witty invention that can catapult humanity, allowing life to be done in a better way.

Love is not something you say but it's what you do.

Love is patient, love is kind. It does not envy, it does not boast, it is not proud. It does not dishonor others, it is not self-seeking, it is not easily angered, it keeps no record of wrongs. Love does not delight in evil but rejoices with the truth. It always protects, always trusts, always hopes, always perseveres.

1 Corinthians 13:4-7 (NIV)

Here's a series of questions to ask yourself:
- Am I patient in developing my giftings?
- Am I kind in my approach to those I come into contact with?
- Am I envious of what other people have or their capabilities and level of gifting?
- Am I boasting about my own accomplishments, giftings, capabilities?
- Do I think proudly my work or calling is more important or better than others?
- Do I honor other people's work, acknowledging their greatness?

- Am I totally concerned about what I can get out of a situation or do I focus on the better of the whole?
- Am I easily angered, annoyed, irritated by others?
- Do I keep a count of other people's trespasses?
- Do I choose to look more at the fallen nature of a person or who God has called them to be?
- Am I giving Godly council, instructions to keep people from the traps of the enemy?
- Do I trust God to listen and obey his voice especially when it contradicts my fallen human nature?
- Do I hope in the best for the future of my family, community, nation or do I let what I see control my feelings and expectations?
- Even in the mist of setbacks, difficulties, misunderstanding and mishaps do I persevere towards the calling of God to make my mark on the world?

Prayer

Father, because you love me, I also love others. I will not allow disappoints, discouragements and evil doings from others to stop me from loving. Open my eyes that I may know my purpose in this life, that I may fulfill it and live in your perfect will: establishing your Kingdom on earth advancing all of humanity in the name of love. Thank you, father, for allowing me to see people as you see them. I choose love, Amen.

Joy

Joy is a supernatural endowment from God.

It's in your assignment from God that you have Joy. You can look externally for joy, but you will only experience momentarily pleasure. God has placed all kinds of skills on the inside of you (Exodus 35:31-32). He takes joy in seeing you become the best version of yourself, displaying those skills to the world (Ephesians 2:10), He loves to see his children unleash potential and create a life of abundance and prosperity, it's a pleasure to him (Psalm 35:27). Likewise, when you release your potential and create that life of abundance and prosperity you receive joy.

It's in doing what you were assigned or created to do that brings joy. You are releasing potential and we are designed to fill that state of joy when we get out of us what God placed in us.

Do you remember the time you learned to ride a bike, you passed the driver's test, or you passed that exam? You were unleashing your potential and it caused Joy to come upon you. Continue to discover who you are, release that potential and you'll find Joy.

Think about this, How do you feel when you are full of joy? Here's my point, Joy allows you to flow in all the other divine characteristics effortlessly.

It's easy to love, have peace, patience, kindness, goodness, faithfulness, gentleness and self-control when you have joy. Joy empowers you to be your divine self, not allowing the fallen human nature to have control.

In thy presence is fulness of joy; at thy right hand there are pleasures for evermore.

Psalm 16:11 (KJV)

Prayer

Father, I take strength in knowing that with you all things are possible. Because all things are possible, I do not limit myself. I act on the assignments that you give me. Thank you for placing potential in me to release to the world to fulfill my assignments, and not leaving me empty, but replacing that released potential with Joy. In Jesus name, I choose Joy Amen.

Peace

Peace is resting in the finished works of Christ.

When we walk closely with God, he multiplies our peace (1 Peter 1:2). Your peace doesn't multiply in the opinions of others or examining your current situation and circumstances, but only through walking continually with the father. When you walk with the father he begins to tell and show you who you were created to be, what you can achieve.

Chaos is walking contrary to God causing a separation, peace is walking with God causing a mutual beneficial relationship!

God has placed in you the treasure, it's only right to give him a return on his investment by innovating, creating, pioneering, cultivating, trailblazing.

You have nothing to be concerned about his peace will be with you.

Peace translated in Hebrew is *Shalom* (harmony, wholeness, completeness, prosperity, welfare, tranquility).

Peace is:
- Nothing missing
- Nothing broken
- Nothing lacking

When you walk with God, you have everything you need to be successful.

> Rejoice in the Lord always [delight, take pleasure in Him]; again, I will say, rejoice! Let your gentle spirit [your graciousness, unselfishness, mercy, tolerance, and patience] be known to all people. The Lord is near. Do not be anxious or worried about anything, but in everything [every circumstance and situation] by prayer and petition with thanksgiving, continue to make your [specific] requests known to God. And the peace of God [that peace which reassures the heart, that peace] which transcends all understanding, [that peace which] stands guard over your hearts and your minds in Christ Jesus [is yours].
> *Philippians 4:4-7 (AMP)*

> Peace I leave with you; my peace I give you. I do not give to you as the world gives. Do not let your hearts be troubled and do not be afraid.
> *John 14:27 (NIV)*

Prayer

Father, because nothing is too hard with you, I have peace, I go boldly towards accomplishing every good work that you have called me to do. I am not trou-bled by the world and its limitations, I stand on your Word, care, anxiety, fear and worry are far from me, your peace is near to me. I choose peace. In Jesus name, Amen.

Long-Suffering

Long-suffering is maintaining your posture on what God said throughout various seasons of life.

Often times we give up on the promises of God and things that we know he has spoken to us to do because we are not aware that long suffering is a key factor in staying in rhythm with the prophetic word we receive and the process of walking it out.

This is the reason why many people never see the prophetic word manifest in their lives. They receive it by faith but over time life has a way of making the prophetic word lose its punch and its kick.

Following through with the plan of God is not an emotional duty. It's a discipline that we must learn. We need to deliver on schedule causing no one to get a delay on their breakthroughs, answers and solutions. You have something to release into the world! Put it on a timetable and get it out there! Work diligently and don't grow weary.

The plans of the diligent lead to profit as surely as haste leads to poverty.

Proverbs 21:5

And let us not be weary in well doing for in due season we shall reap, if we faint not.

Galatians 6:9

Success comes from repeatedly and consistently applying yourself. You should be applying yourself daily, in the many areas of your life in order to breakthrough into untrotted paths. A breakthrough is when one leaves the level, they are currently on to advance and go to another level, to an undiscovered place that will force them to tap into their unleashed potential. Breakthroughs reveal to you what you are capable of (Philippians 4:13).

Scientists, doctors, educators are always studying and looking to improve the systems in which they are a part of. When they discover a new, more efficient and effective way of operating they call it a breakthrough. So, we have scientific breakthroughs, medical breakthroughs, educational breakthroughs, all in which require long suffering in the process of leaving what is here and now and going to the undiscovered, the unleashed.

You can have breakthrough as well, you can breakthrough and discover the many facets to who you are. There is so much about you that you have yet to discover. Make it your life's mission to discover the person

God foreknew and predestined to do great and mighty things in the world. Long-suffering is vital in doing so, so that you stay in the game, seeing your mission out until the end.

Prayer

Father, thank you for your plan for my life, I receive it now and not grow weary in the process of it coming from one realm into another. I conduct my life's affairs according to your plan. I understand that if I am diligent, I will get results. I praise you now that my life shows that your ways bring good results. I choose long-suffering, in Jesus name, Amen.

Gentleness

Gentleness provokes unity and welcomes brotherhood causing great manifestation of vision through teamwork.

It's hard to work in an environment with people who are not pleasant to be around. As glory carriers we shouldn't be the one that people don't want to interact with. In fact, if we are to get our purpose done, potential out, vision moving, and God's intent established it's going to require us working with people.

In Genesis 11 the people were all on one accord flowing in unity. They had one mind and one language and because of this they were able to begin building a tower up to heaven as they purposed in their hearts.

And the Lord said, Behold, they are one people and they have one language; and this is only the beginning of what they will do, and now nothing they have imagined they can do will be impossible for them.

Genesis 11:6 (AMP)

Can you imagine the gentleness they shared with one another to make each other feel valuable, important, worthy of the cause? We must take on the same mindset that these people had as it relates to building a team. They had a vison of a tower up to heaven but before the tower could be built, they had to build a team that would work together, be reliable, feel appreciated, had encouragement and support. They built the team by using the spirit of gentleness.

The opposing side of gentleness would be confusion and a lack of communication. This is how God stopped the people from building the tower to heaven. He confused their language, he made it where they couldn't communicate with one another properly.

Operating in the spirit of gentleness carries skills. The people being gentle as well as the people receiving the gentleness from others begin to flow in the following skills:

- Time management skills
- Mind-management skills
- Leadership skills
- Effective communication skills
- Negotiation skills

- Crisis management skills
- Change management skills
- Resource management skills
- Trailblazing skills

All these skills are needed to build your vision.

Let your gentle spirit [your graciousness, unselfishness, mercy, tolerance, and patience] be known to all people. The Lord is near.

Philippians 4:5 (AMP)

A soft and gentle and thoughtful answer turns away wrath, but harsh and painful and careless words stir up anger.

Proverbs 15:1 (AMP)

Prayer
Father, as I study your Word allow it to inspire, edify and build me up. As the Word constructs me in such manner, cause the spirit of Gentleness to come upon me so that I may inspire, edify and build up those I encounter. I refuse to be judgmental or make accusations, but I will give the same acceptance that has been given to me. I have one focus and that is to release everything you've put on the inside of me, and I won't allow confusion and poor communication to stop me from displaying your creative work in the systems of the world. In Jesus name, I choose gentleness, Amen.

Goodness

Goodness shares all good things.

Releasing your potential is good but what really is good is releasing it for the good of other people. You shouldn't want to release your potential just for the sake of looking good and celebrity status which is rightfully yours as a son or daughter of the King (garment of praise) but to push humanity forward.

Goodness does not look to self-gratify but it looks to meet moral and integral standards of the Kingdom of God, which is to spread the good news across the world so that people will be saved, delivered, set free and whole.

Goodness allows us to conduct our affairs in the most upright, noble, pure and virtuous way, being in God's perfect will, far from evil which is anything out of God's will.

> Do not be overcome and conquered by evil but overcome evil with good.
>
> *Romans 12:21*

Prayer

My father and my God, thank you for the goodness you allow to follow me each day. You are good to me, I will reflect your goodness by being good to others by walking out the call of God for my life in boldness, sufficiency, effectiveness and excellency. I am a distributor of your goodness, thank you for withholding no good thing from me. I choose goodness, in Jesus name, Amen.

Faith

Faith is the connector to the promises of God.

If you are going to be a purpose driven individual, then you are going to have to also be a person that walks by faith. In the natural you may not be qualified to carry out your vision or God's plan for your life. You will not be able to see with your natural eyes what God desires for your life. You have to open your spiritual eyes and see in the realm of the Spirit.

The spirit realm is the casual realm, what this means is that everything that comes into existence that we can see with our natural eyes must first be seen with spiritual eyes.

Before your greatness is released in all the earth, you have to connect with the source of your greatness, which is God. Faith then begins to go in full operation, and you begin to walk out the life that God showed you.

So, then faith cometh by hearing, and hearing by the Word of God.

Romans 10:17 (KJV)

We have to continue in the Word of God in order to remain disciplined to walk out our life with purpose (John 8:33).

Now faith is the assurance (the confirmation, the title deed) of the things [we] hope for, being the proof of things [we] do not see and the conviction of their reality [faith perceiving as real fact what is not revealed to the senses].

Hebrews 11:1

The spirit realm is the casual realm, it is realer than the natural realm. You don't get a manifestation in the natural without a mediation in the Spirit.

Prayer
Father, I decree and declare that I look to you alone. My faith is in your Word. I dismantle any thoughts, ideas or suggestions that I have placed above your precepts and I repent. I will say only what you have said, think only your thoughts, and do what you do, because of my faith. I choose faith in Jesus name, Amen.

Self-control

Self-control protects your life.

God gives us the spirit of self-control that we will resist the temptation that comes to take us off our course of establishing his Kingdom on earth. The temptation of fear, worries, burning passions, and lustful desires can cause us to forfeit our inheritance.

We must bring order into our lives, if we are going to have self-control.

Areas to bring order:
- Home life
- Friendships

- Business partners
- Work environment
- Associations and acquaintances

The places you spend most of your time and the people you work with and associate with on a consist basis need to understand boundaries.

Boundaries protect a person's body, thoughts, feelings and spirit. We should always keep guard of these areas for they dictate to your heart the course of your life (Proverbs 4:23).

When people cross boundaries we put ourselves in a place where we are vulnerable to backsliding. Backsliding is returning to old strategies, methodologies and technologies when God has elevated us to a new paradigm where we can work smarter, doing more in less time.

In order to set boundaries, you need to know your temptations (James 1:14). You need to pray about those temptations (Luke 22:40) and you need to ask God to guide you from them (Luke 11:4).

Attack the enemy with the sword of the spirt which is the Word of God and he will leave from among you (James 4:7). This is what Jesus himself had to do during his time of temptation by the devil trying to destroy his mission, purpose and assignment from God the father.

Read Luke 4:1-14.

Jesus operated with self-control. He couldn't control the enemy, but he could control himself by releasing what God the father had already declared over his life.

Like a city that is broken down and without walls [leaving it unprotected] Is a man who has no self-control over his spirit [and sets himself up for trouble].

Proverbs 25:28

God did not give us a spirit of timidity or cowardice or fear, but [He has given us a spirit] of power and of love and of sound judgment and personal discipline [abilities that result in a calm, well-balanced mind and self-control].

2 Timothy 1:7

Prayer

My father and my God, I thank you that my self-control is not done in my own power or strength but through your Word. Your Word gives me direction and it affords me the ability to fight back the devil when he brings temptations. Father, open my eyes that I may see the wiles of the enemy coming to me in temptation form, In Jesus name, I choose self-discipline, Amen.

MEEKNESS

Meekness brings about acceleration.

A meek person is a person that operates in the anointing that the disciples operated in which is the anointing for learning.

For you to be all that God has called you to be, you are going to have to be a learner and willing to submit to authority. Authority being anyone that holds some knowledge, wisdom and understanding in an area that you don't but it's vital for your success. You may be more qualified than they are, your assignment may be greater, you may know more than them in other areas, make more money but if you're going to release hidden potential, submission is going to be required.

So many people settle for mediocre lives because they don't want to submit. Submitting is not a weakness or the act of unintelligence. Intelligent people submit.

Submissiveness causes you to get more done faster, it causes you to know the possible detours and plan accordingly when on the journey towards destiny. You can't say that you want to be taught, trained or mentored but you don't take heed to what the teacher or mentor is saying. God places people in our lives who can equip us with what we need to see our greatness manifest (1 Corinthians 4:17).

You can gain success faster through learning from individuals rather than learning through actual experience because that can take years to learn and deal with the aftermath, which wastes your time. The time needed to fulfill purpose.

The ultimate teacher and mentor is the Holy Spirit (John 14:26), (Luke 12:12), (Nehemiah 9:20).

Therefore, it's important to develop that relationship because he will lead and guide you into all truth concerning your life and destiny (John 16:13), keeping you from wasting your time. You will have a peace that you will not be able to articulate (Philippians 4:7) because only he knows the beginning from the ending (Isaiah 46:10), and you'll be connected to him therefore he'll let you know things concerning your dealings in the earth. Life will not or doesn't not have to be a mystery to you.

The meek shall inherit the earth; and shall delight themselves in the abundance of peace.

Psalm 37:11

Prayer

Father, I declare that my spirit is open to your instructions. Let there be no interference from what you are saying from heaven to earth concerning me. I humble myself before you lord, I am willing to receive the overwhelming overflow of revelation that will cause me to do the impossible, send me the right mentors, instructors and tutors needed to help me become all you created me to be. I choose meekness. In Jesus name, Amen.

Putting it into perspective

Understanding your divine character will not only strengthen your fellowship with the father but It is the fruit of the Spirit that develops your potential, releases your earthy treasure and sustains your success.

Beware of false prophets, who come to you dressed as sheep, but inside they are devouring wolves. You will fully recognize them by their fruits. Do people pick grapes from thorns, or figs from thistles? Even so, every healthy (sound) tree bears good fruit [worthy of admiration], but the sickly (decaying, worthless) tree bears bad (worthless) fruit. A good (healthy) tree cannot bear bad (worthless) fruit, nor can a bad (diseased) tree bear excellent fruit [worthy of admiration]. Every tree that does not bear good fruit is cut down and cast into the fire. Therefore, you will fully know them by their fruits

Matthew 7:15-20

By now you can see the vitalness of baring the fruit of the Spirit, which is the characteristics of Christ, the anointed one. If you don't have the character, then you cannot manifest God's nature through your daily interactions and affairs of life.

The proof is the fruit!

Are you a creature of your divine nature?

Therefore if anyone is in Christ [that is, grafted in, joined to Him by faith in Him as Savior], he is a new creature [reborn and renewed by the Holy Spirit]; the old things [the previous moral and spiritual condition] have passed away. Behold, new things have come [because spiritual awakening brings a new life].

2 Corinthians 5:17

Imitate God, therefore, in everything you do, because you are his dear children.

Ephesians 5:1

And show your own self in all respects to be a pattern and a model of good deeds and works, teaching what is unadulterated, showing gravity [having the strictest regard for truth and purity of motive], with dignity and seriousness. And let your instruction be sound and fit and wise and wholesome, vigorous and irrefutable and above censure, so that the opponent may be put to shame, finding nothing discrediting or evil to say about us.

Titus 2:7-8

Faith without Kingdom correspondence is dead (James 2:17). Without Kingdom correspondence we are performing and not ministering, hyping but not changing. Operating in your divine nature, character is corresponding your actions with what you believe. To be successful in life you must have singleness of mind, you must focus solely on your divine nature by thinking and doing as you believe. Without your thoughts and actions in alignment you will be unstable being not fit for God's presence (James 1:8).

Not everyone who says to Me, 'Lord, Lord,' will enter the kingdom of heaven, but only he who does the will of My Father who is in heaven. Many will say to Me on that day [when I judge them], 'Lord, Lord, have we not prophesied in Your name, and driven out demons in Your name, and done many miracles in Your name?' And then I will declare to them publicly, 'I never knew you; DEPART FROM ME [you are banished from My presence], YOU WHO ACT WICKEDLY [disregarding My commands].'

Matthew 7:21-23

Jesus said to him, I am the Way and the Truth and the Life; no one comes to the Father except by (through) Me.

John 14:6

If someone claims, "I know him well!" but doesn't keep his commandments, he's obviously a liar. His life doesn't match his words. But the one who keeps God's Word is the person in whom we see God's mature love. This is the only way to be sure we're in God. Anyone who claims to be intimate with God ought to live the same kind of life Jesus lived.

1 John 2:4-6

He that saith, I know him, and keepeth not his commandments, is a liar, and the truth is not in him. But whoso keepeth his word, in him verily is the love of God perfected: hereby know we that we are in him. He that saith he abideth in him ought himself also so to walk, even as he walked.

1 John 2:4-6

Living life through your divine nature allows you to walk in accordance to God's commands, perfecting you and making you able to accomplish great things. It is what Integrity is all about, being who you were created to be and being true to that person. To live any life outside of your divine nature is to live a lie and a life beneath your privileges. You should live life as your authentic self in all interactions to display the unlimited glories of God.

There is power in your choices. Choose to live life through your divine human nature instead of the fallen human nature.

Choose:
- Love over hate
- Joy over depression
- Peace over conflict
- Patience over frustration
- Kindness over meanness
- Goodness over wickedness
- Faithfulness over being uncommitted
- Gentleness over harshness
- Self-control over lack of discipline

Chapter 4

✝

CHANGE OF ATTITUDE

*It is your attitude, more than your aptitude,
that will determine your altitude.
– Zig Ziglar*

We've talked about your unleashed potential. In this particular chapter, I want to begin to discuss your attitude. You can have all the potential in the world to live a successful and prosperous life (which you do) but without the correct attitude, you will never experience it.

You can alter your life, by simply altering your attitude. Your attitude is more important than your skills, talents, capabilities and competence. This is what Jesus message was exclusively about on the Mount in the gospel of Matthew.

Through evaluation it's been proven that sickness, divorce, money shortage and troublesome children are consistent in a person's life with a faulty attitude. Most people are laboring under a huge misconception.

Misconception: "I can't help the way I feel. That's just the way I am." The truth is that you can change the way you feel. Your attitudes are totally changeable and controllable.

Before we explore Jesus teaching on the Mount, I want to show you a research study that validates the fact that your attitude determines your aptitude.

Research Study:

Out of 1500 people, 83% (group A) of them took their particular jobs because of money, 17% (group B) took their jobs because of the love of the job.

After 20 years, 101 out of the 1500 people were millionaires. The amazing thing is only one of those millionaires came from the 83% (group A) that worked for just money, but 100 of them came from the 17% (group B). Over 70% of those millionaires NEVER went to college. And over 70% of those who became CEO's graduated in the BOTTOM HALF of their class. This concluded that it was their attitude, more than their aptitude, which determined their altitude.

JESUS' STANCE ON ATTITUDE

What makes this message from Jesus so exceptional is not only the message within itself but the locality of the message. He taught it on a mountain which exhibits elevation, altitude. The very thing that his message if applied by the listeners would bring into their lives. Let's now unfold his message of the attitudes we should live with so that we will live blessed lives, empowered to be successful and prosperous.

Attitude One: Humility

You're blessed when you're at the end of your rope. With less of you there is more of God and his rule.
Blessed are the poor in spirit: for theirs is the kingdom of heaven.

Matthew 5:3

Being poor in spirit is opposite of self-sufficiency. People who are poor in spirit realize that they are in total helplessness and lost apart from God, our father.

My sacrifice [the sacrifice acceptable] to God is a broken spirit; a broken and a contrite heart [broken down with sorrow for sin and humbly and thoroughly penitent], such, O God, you will not despise.

Psalm 51:17

Attitude Two: Repentance

You're blessed when you feel you've lost what is most dear to you. Only then can you be embraced by the One most dear to you.

Blessed are they that mourn for they shall be comforted.

Matthew 5:4

Here Jesus is speaking about those who mourn over their sin. A mourning over your sin is a Godly sorrow that produces repentance and leads to realignment with God's will. Godly sorrow affects a person down into their soul. There is a deep agony because one knows they haven't followed the principals and prescribed patterns from Father God.

When King David sinned when he had an affair with Bathsheba and had her husband killed, he felt sorrow, remorse, guilt and shame. He mourned over what he had done. The betrayal to God.

Against You, you only, have I sinned and done that which is evil in Your sight, So that You are justified when You speak [Your sentence] and faultless in Your judgment.

Psalm 51:4

If we confess our sins, he is faithful and just to forgive us our sins, and to cleanse us from all unrighteousness.

1 John 1:9

Attitude Three: Teachability

You're blessed when you are content with just who you are—no more, no less. That's the moment you find yourselves proud owners of everything that can't be bought.
Blessed are the meek: for they shall inherit the earth.
Matthew 5:5

In the original language, "meek" is used in bridling a horse or taming a wild animal. This is a picture of power, under control. So, a meek person is one who's life has been brought under influence of the Holy Spirit, and God is in control of their life.
We are to drive our own lives but allow God to be the navigator.
The meek are sensitive to the divine will of God.
The meek are not easily provoked or irritated.
The meek are not proud, self-sufficient, or stubborn.
The meek are not unmanageable or ill-tempered.
Jesus himself was meek.

So, Jesus explained himself at length. "I'm telling you this straight. The Son can't independently do a thing, only what he sees the Father doing. What the Father does, the Son does. The Father loves the Son and includes him in everything he is doing.
John 1:19-20

Here Jesus was speaking to the Jewish leaders who came against him for healing on the sabbath and then putting himself on the same level with God by saying God is his father.

Jesus willingness to be like the father and obedient to his commands made him meek. He didn't let tradition, custom and normality keep him from being groomed by God.

Meekness is self-control empowered by the Holy Spirit.

Jesus' encounter at the temple with the money exchangers was not him being provoked, irritated, ill-tempered or unmanageable emotionally but rather provoked, moved, managed by the Father to do so based on his meekness.

We need to be sensitive to the will of God and the power of the Holy Spirit. We need to be submissive enough that we don't hesitate when he tells us to act, no matter how foolish it may seem or uncultured it appears to be.

Attitude Four: Righteousness

Blessed [joyful, nourished by God's goodness] are those who hunger and thirst for righteousness [those who actively seek right standing with God], for they will be [completely] satisfied.

Matthew 5:6

We need to have the same righteous desires as God. We should stand for what he stands for, stand against what he stands against.

Our passion, our driving hunger needs to be on those things that are pleasing to God. In laymen's terms this would be your assignment and purpose. Being in right standing isn't just about keeping his laws but being obedient to the call and the mandate that he has given you.

Let's look at what Moses said.

> For I will proclaim the name [and presence] of the Lord. Concede and ascribe greatness to our God. He is the Rock, His work is perfect, for all His ways are law and justice. A God of faithfulness without breach or deviation, just and right is He.
>
> *Deuteronomy 32:3-4*

The desire for righteousness should drive our lives. God wants us to have such a desire for him and his ways that without it, it's like starvation hunger.

This is the reason many people are in a perplex cycle of unsatisfaction. They buy everything to fill a void that only fulfilling purpose and being in right standing with God can fill. So, their closets are filled to capacity, garage is filled to capacity, but they are still fragmented.

If we hunger and thirst after the things of God we will be satisfied, material things get old and we will want the new hit, but the righteousness of God never gets old, it's continually evolving us, progressing us and advancing us. We cannot live without it, or should I say we can't afford to live without it!

Attitude Five: Mercy

> Blessed are the merciful: for they shall obtain mercy.
> *Matthew 5:6*

God demonstrates forgiveness and mercy to us freely. The way we receive we should give. FREELY (Matthew 10:8).

The manner in which we forgive, we will be forgiven and we need a lot of forgiveness.

> And forgive us our debts, as we forgive our debtors.
> *Matthew 6:12*

> For all have sinned and fallen short of the Glory of God.
> *Romans 3:23*

Attitude Six: Purity

> Blessed are the pure at heart, for they will see God.
> *Matthew 5:8*

In the Greek the word pure has many facets.
It was used to describe dirty clothes that had been washed clean as well as grain and flour that had been

carefully sifted. It also was used to describe milk or wine that had not been mixed with any other liquid. It had not been diluted or watered down but pure.

Given those Greek insights, it is safe to say that this attitude can be translated, "Blessed is the man who is genuine, uncontaminated and his authentic self for he will see God."

If one is pure, one is holy. It does not mean one is perfect but striving to be clean and bringing their thoughts, emotions and actions all in agreement with God's Word.

Paul wrote to Timothy: "Flee the evil desires of youth and pursue righteousness, faith, love and peace, along with those who call on the LORD out of a pure heart (Timothy 2:22)."

A person with a pure heart is one that is not contaminated but lives as God has created them to live life with these 40 qualities.

Qualities of a pure heart:
1. Awareness
2. Godliness
3. Truth
4. Commitment
5. Patience
6. Capacity
7. Wholeness
8. Balance
9. Peace
10. Goodness

11. Discipline
12. Simplicity
13. Uniqueness
14. Passion
15. Joy
16. Beauty
17. Effortlessness
18. Authenticity
19. Focus
20. Order
21. Faith
22. Gratitude
23. Destiny
24. Identity
25. Purpose
26. Integrity
27. Responsibility
28. Potential
29. Impeccability
30. Compassion
31. Respect
32. Loyalty
33. Credibility
34. Temperance
35. Morality
36. Justice
37. Tolerance
38. Ethics
39. Interdependence
40. Community

Attitude Seven: Peacemaking

> Blessed are the peacemakers, for they will be called children of God.
> *Matthew 5:9*

As followers of Christ we should be peacemakers, not peace breakers. We should be a part of the solution, not the problem. We should be peacemakers in our homes, church, workplace, in our communities and wherever we must conduct our affairs.

Here is a prime example of being a peace maker, demonstrated by Jesus.

> And when he was entered into a ship, his disciples followed him. And, behold, there arose a great tempest in the sea, insomuch that the ship was covered with the waves: but he was asleep. And his disciples came to him, and awoke him, saying, LORD, save us: we perish. And he saith unto them, Why are ye fearful, O ye of little faith? Then he arose, and rebuked the winds and the sea; and there was a great calm.
> *Matthew 8:23-26*

No matter how big or scary the storm may appear the power to bring peace is within us. Storms attack our lives in many ways but if we remain calm, not fearful and stand in faith God will see us through.

Up to this point, the attitudes that we've discovered focused on humility, meekness, right relationships, mercy, purity, and peacemaking. All of them are positive attitudes. The last and final attitude may not seem so positive and rewarding but Jesus teaches us that we are still blessed.

Attitude Eight: Courage for Persecution

God blesses those who are persecuted for doing right, for the Kingdom of Heaven is theirs.
Matthew 5:10

Because we live in a fallen world the reality is that many will reject us for following righteousness, aligning ourselves with God's perspective and viewpoint. Jesus pushes the point further by mentioning that the prophets, who like him announced God's Kingdom, were persecuted.

Persecution simply comes to put an end to the move of God by oppressing the people who are pushing the agenda of God's Kingdom on earth, those that are standing for what's right.

God is faithful and he will not allow our good for his mission to be trampled over by men.

Then my enemies will see that the LORD is on my side. They will be ashamed that they taunted me, saying, "So where is the LORD— that God of yours?" With my own eyes I will see their downfall; they will be trampled like mud in the streets.
Micah 7:10

It's Your Season

> You are the salt of the earth. But what good is salt if it has lost its flavor? Can you make it salty again? It will be thrown out and trampled underfoot as worthless.
>
> *Matthew 5:13*

It's our duty as born-again believers to confess and demonstrate the works of Christ. When we do so we are bringing flavor, to the dry parts of this world. Dry, meaning unproductive because there is no anointing flowing. So, when you begin to stand for what's right, you release God's anointing on earth and where God's anointing is, burdens are removed and yokes are destroyed (scripture).

He is no fool who follows God, no matter the persecution.

Choose to develop these unstoppable forces of attitudes vs. attitudes that hinder, stagnate and bring division causing you not to reach your goals, maximize your potential and fulfill your assignments.

Choose:
- Humility over pride
- Repentance over stubbornness
- Teachability over being uncooperative and self-willed
- Righteousness over unrighteousness
- Mercy over ruthlessness
- Purity over contamination
- Peacemaking over fighting
- Courage over being timid

Weakness of attitude becomes weakness of character.
— Albert Einstein

Nothing can stop the man with the right mental attitude from achieving his goal; nothing on earth can help a man with the wrong mental attitude.
— Thomas Jefferson

Chapter 5

✝

THE FATHER'S IDENTITY

*The people that do know their God shall
be strong, and do exploits.
Daniel 11:32*

It is very important to know the father's identity. It reveals his assignment and what he has done, allowing us to better know his nature. It's imperative that we know his nature so that we can hold fast to the truth of the reminder in Hebrews 13:5 that God will never leave us nor forsake us. When we know the truth of, he'll never leave us or forsake us we will have strength in our life's circumstances, and we will be able to do exploits. Exploits meaning daring deeds, having success against all odds, accomplishing greatness.

Jehovah is translated as "The existing one" or "Lord". It comes from the Hebrew word *havah*, meaning "to be" or "to exist". It also suggests "to be known" this indicates a God who reveals himself unceasingly, in many areas and circumstances.

And God said unto Moses, I AM THAT I AM: and he said, Thus shall you say unto the children of Israel, I AM has sent me unto you.
Exodus 3:14 (KJV)

"I the LORD do not change. So, you, the descendants of Jacob, are not destroyed.
Malachi 3:6 (NIV)

The LORD God Almighty, the LORD is his name!
Hosea 12:5 (NIV)

John, To the seven churches in the province of Asia: Grace and peace to you from him who is, and who was, and who is to come, and from the seven spirits before his throne.
Revelation 1:4

I am the Alpha and the Omega," says the LORD God, "who is, and who was, and who is to come, the Almighty."
Revelation 1:8

God cannot be put in a box. By getting to know his identity, you'll began to realize just how unstoppable he is. He is the ultimate problem solver! He is a GREAT GOD! When he shows up, be brings RESULTS, and that's what we all want, right?

It's imperative to know that God is:
- Sovereign (Supreme, highest)
- Holy (Set apart)
- Omniscient (All knowing, all seeing)

EL, ELOAH [el, el-oh-ah]: God mighty, strong, prominent

ELOHIM [el-oh-heem]: God Creator, sustainer, supreme judge

EL SHADDAI [el-shah-dahy]: God Almighty, who nourishes, supplies, satis-fies

EL-OLAM [el-oh-lahm]: Everlasting God

EL ROI [el-roh-ee]: God of Seeing, knows all

The Identity of the Father

Jehovah Jireh – The Lord who Provides

Now after these things, God tested [the faith and commitment of] Abraham and said to him, "Abraham!" And he answered, "Here I am." God said, "Take now your son, your only son [of promise], whom you love, Isaac, and go to the region of Moriah, and offer him there as a burnt offering on one of the mountains of which I shall tell you." So Abraham got up early in the morning, saddled his donkey, and took two of his young men with him and his son Isaac; and he split the wood for the burnt offering, and then he got up and went to the place of which God had told him. On the third day [of travel] Abraham looked up and saw the place in the distance. Abraham said to his servants, "Settle down and stay here with the donkey; the young man and I will go over there and worship [God], and we will come back to you." Then Abraham took the wood for the burnt offering and laid it on [the shoulders of] Isaac his son, and he took the fire (firepot) in his own hand and the [sacrificial] knife; and the two of them walked on together. And Isaac said to Abraham, "My father!" And he said, "Here I am, my son." Isaac said, "Look, the fire and the wood, but where is the lamb for the burnt offering?" Abraham said, "My son, God will provide for Himself a lamb for the burnt offering." So the two walked on together.

When they came to the place of which God had told him, Abraham built an altar there and arranged the wood, and bound Isaac his son and placed him on the altar, on top of the wood. Abraham reached out his hand and took the knife to kill his son. But the Angel of the LORD called to him from heaven and said, "Abraham, Abraham!" He answered, "Here I am." The LORD said, "Do not reach out [with the knife in] your hand against the boy, and do nothing to [harm] him; for now I know that you fear God [with reverence and profound respect], since you have not withheld from Me your son, your only son [of promise]." Then Abraham looked up and glanced around, and behold, behind him was a ram caught in a thicket by his horns. And Abraham went and took the ram and offered it up for a burnt offering (ascending sacrifice) instead of his son. So Abraham named that place The LORD Will Provide. And it is said to this day, "On the mountain of the LORD it will be seen and provided."

Genesis 22:1-14

Notice that provision was made because Abraham was where God told him to be. God did not make provision for something that was outside of his will and plans for Abraham.

We must not think that we can do whatever we want and expect God to put his stamp of approval on it. If it's God's will, then it's God's bill. Where the Lord sends you, he will provide for you. It important to know God's plans concerning your life. We can know his plans by engaging in a personal relationship with him.

Jehovah Rapha- The Lord who heals

"If you will diligently listen and pay attention to the voice of the LORD your God, and do what is right in His sight, and listen to His commandments, and keep [foremost in your thoughts and actively obey] all His precepts and statutes, then I will not put on you any of the diseases which I have put on the Egyptians; for I am the LORD who heals you."

Exodus 15:26

It is not God's will for us to be sick, physically or soulishly (emotionally, psychologically). Therefore, we should know that sickness is not a part of God's divine plan for our life. For this to be a natural reality we must follow the prerequisites found in Exodus 15:26 for both physical and soulish health.

Prerequisites:
- (Pray)Listen/pay attention to voice of God
- (Have his perspective) Do what's right in his sight
- (Obey)Listen to his commandments, keep his precepts and statutes

Jehovah Shammah- The Lord who is present

Read Ezekiel 40.

Ezekiel describes a temple that would be built in the future. He prophesies that the Lord will be there.

In Isaiah 2:2 Isaiah speaks of a house of the Lord that he saw through a vision.

And it shall come to pass in the last days, that the mountain of the LORD's house shall be established in the top of the mountains, and shall be exalted above the hills; and all nations shall flow unto it.

Isaiah 2:2

Do you not know that your bodies are temples of the Holy Spirit, who is in you, whom you have received from God? You are not your own; you were bought at a price. Therefore honor God with your bodies.

1 Corinthians 6:19-20

Can I submit to you that we are the temples that were prophesied about by Ezekiel and Isaiah? God's presence, his attendance in your life is not limited to a brick and mortar building or a geographical location.

Then Peter said unto them, Repent, and be baptized every one of you in the name of Jesus Christ for the remission of sins, and ye shall receive the gift of the Holy Ghost.

Acts 2:38

When a person is baptized into Christ, they receive the gift of the Holy Spirit, which is his spirit. At that point our bodies become the dwelling place for the Holy Spirit, or in other words God's presence.

Like in building a brick and mortar temple, our bodies are designed to glorify God and not participate in sin. We must live a consecrated life. A life of consecration is a life where God is present, and his works are made known through our day to day interactions.

Jehovah Shalom- The Lord of Peace

And he said unto him, Oh my Lord, wherewith shall I save Israel? behold, my family is poor in Manasseh, and I am the least in my father's house. And the LORD said unto him, Surely I will be with thee, and thou shalt smite the Midianites as one man. And he said unto him, If now I have found grace in thy sight, then shew me a sign that thou talkest with me. Depart not hence, I pray thee, until I come unto thee, and bring forth my present, and set it before thee. And he said, I will tarry until thou come again. And Gideon went in, and made ready a kid, and unleavened cakes of an ephah of flour: the flesh he put in a basket, and he put the broth in a pot, and brought it out unto him under the oak, and presented it. And the angel of God said unto him, Take the flesh and the unleavened cakes, and lay them upon this rock, and pour out the broth. And he did so Then the angel of the LORD put forth the end of the staff that was in his hand, and touched the flesh and the unleavened cakes; and there rose up fire out of the rock, and consumed the flesh and the unleavened cakes. Then the angel of the LORD departed out of his sight. And when Gideon perceived that he was an angel of the LORD, Gideon said, Alas, O LORD God! for because I have seen an angel of the LORD face to face. And the LORD said unto him, Peace be unto thee; fear not: thou shalt not die Then Gideon built an altar there unto the LORD, and called it Jehovah shalom.

Judges 6:13-24

In some very dark hours of Israel's history God revealed himself to Gideon as Jehovah Shalom. When the hour is dark, we are desperate and we are brought low, we long to know that all will be well. We seek for peace.

That is, that God was in Christ reconciling the world to Himself, not counting people's sins against them [but canceling them]. And He has committed to us the message of reconciliation [that is, restoration to favor with God].

2 Corinthians 5:19

For to us a Child shall be born, to us a Son shall be given; and the government shall be upon His shoulder, and His name shall be called Wonderful Counselor, Mighty God, Everlasting Father, Prince of Peace.

Isaiah 9:6

For I know the plans I have for you," declares the LORD, "plans to prosper you and not to harm you, plans to give you hope and a future.

Jeremiah 29:11

And, having made peace through the blood of his cross, by him to reconcile all things unto himself; by him, I say, whether they be things in earth, or things in heaven.

Colossians 1:20

God sent Jesus to bring us back to a state of peace. Nothing missing, nothing broken or nothing lacking. We are WHOLE, through the works of Jesus.

Jehovah Nissi- The Lord our Banner

Read Exodus 17.

When Israel came up against the Amalekites in battle at Rephidim it wasn't with this great and mighty natural force. They didn't have an experienced army or the top of the line commanders. They were a tribe of herdsmen escaping slavery in Egypt who were traveling to a promise land that hadn't been seen in over 400years. They were a group of women, children, herds and their possessions traveling through a land of trained fierce fighting people.

This battle that they fought is a battle similar to the battles that we face today, for survival, hope and a future.

Let's remember all that God has done for them before this point. This will help us to understand that they traveled with a pillar of smoke of fire, a cloud of smoke, the very presence of God.

If Jehovah Shammah was with them, he brought them to the land, although they were inexperienced or overmatched, they were never the underdogs. They were VICTORIOUS!

Victorious indeed, they overcame what appeared to be much more than they could handle. This was the first time that God showed them as a nation that he fought for them, that he led them in battle, that he protected and conquered on their behalf.

The question now arises, what does it mean for God to be our banner? To answer this question, we must consider how banners are used.

Banners are visible, made to be seen. Unmistakable and unignorable. Banners are for those raising them and those who view them.

We are to celebrate and honor God's faithfulness, remember his deeds, live for him as ambassadors.

The Lord our banner is not just telling who God is or what he has done but who we are as a people who follow and hearken to his voice. We are VICTORIOUS!

Jehovah Rohi- The Lord my Shepherd

The LORD is my shepherd; I shall not want. He maketh me to lie down in green pastures: he leadeth me beside the still waters. He restoreth my soul: he leadeth me in the paths of righteousness for his name's sake. Yea, though I walk through the valley of the shadow of death, I will fear no evil: for thou art with me; thy rod and thy staff they comfort me. Thou preparest a table before me in the presence of mine enemies: thou anointest my head with oil; my cup run-neth over.6 Surely goodness and mercy shall follow me all the days of my life: and I will dwell in the house of the LORD forever.

Psalm 23

This is a very familiar passage of scripture but what does it really mean?

If the Lord is our shepherd, we must look at ourselves as sheep. Sheep need shepherds, for they have a natural tendency to wander off and get lost.

All of us like sheep have gone astray, we have turned, each one, to his own way; but the LORD has caused the wickedness of us all [our sin, our injustice, our wrongdoing] to fall on Him [instead of us].

Isaiah 53:6

Believers are the same way as sheep. When sheep go astray, they are in danger of getting lost, being attacked, killing themselves by drowning or falling off cliffs.

When we don't stay close to the Word of God, we will live a defeated life, following after sin, approaching life in the wrong way.

When we were living in the flesh [trapped by sin], the sinful passions, which were awakened by [that which] the Law [identifies as sin], were at work in our body to bear fruit for death [since the willingness to sin led to death and separation from God].

Romans 7:5

And those who are in the flesh [living a life that caters to sinful appetites and impulses] cannot please God.

Romans 8:8

For all that is in the world—the lust and sensual craving of the flesh and the lust and longing of the eyes and the boastful pride of life [pretentious confidence in one's resources or in the stability of earthly things]—these do not come from the Father, but are from the world.

1 John 2:16

For this reason [that is, because of God's final revelation in His Son Jesus and because of Jesus' superiority to the angels] we must pay much closer attention than ever to the things that we have heard, so that we do not [in any way] drift away from truth.

Hebrews 2:1

It is our fallen human nature to drift away, to reject God, and break his precepts and not follow his principals, or to go after righteousness. When we follow our fallen human nature, the risk becomes getting lost, soon finding ourselves confronting the enemy time and time again, placing us in survival mode instead of thriving in life. You were created to thrive, not survive.

Sheep are helpless creatures who cannot survive long without a shepherd. We should be totally dependent on the Lord to guide, protect and care for us.

I have just two questions to ask you. Respond honestly and develop a plan to change your answer if it is one that is undesirable.

Are you the sheep of Jesus?
Is Jesus your Shepheard?

Jesus answered them, "I have told you so, yet you do not believe. The works that I do in My Father's name testify concerning Me [they are My credentials and the evidence declaring who I am]. But you do not believe Me [so you do not trust and follow Me] because you are not My sheep. The sheep that are My own hear My voice and listen to Me; I know them, and they follow Me. And I give them eternal life, and they will never, ever [by any means] perish; and no one will ever snatch them out of My hand.

John 10:25-28

Jehovah Tsidkenu- The Lord our righteousness

In his days Judah shall be saved, and Israel shall dwell safely: and this is his name whereby he shall be called, The Lord Our Righteousness.
Jeremiah 23:6

We cannot earn righteousness, because of what Jesus did we are made the righteousness of God for this reason it is important to accept Jesus into our lives.

But it is from Him that you are in Christ Jesus, who became to us wisdom from God [revealing His plan of salvation], and righteousness [making us acceptable to God], and sanctification [making us holy and setting us apart for God], and redemption [providing our ransom from the penalty for sin].
1 Corinthians 1:30

He made Christ who knew no sin to [judicially] be sin on our behalf, so that in Him we would become the righteousness of God [that is, we would be made acceptable to Him and placed in a right relationship with Him by His gracious lovingkindness].
2 Corinthians 5:21

We don't have to perform works or keep commandments for the sake of being righteous. We live right and obey God out of Love and thanksgiving for what he brought to us through the works of Jesus. The Word of God Is our training manual on how to live the righteous life that Christ has given us and for growing not more righteous because we are as righteous as we will ever be but growing in Christlikeness, in word, thought and action. Conforming to his image.

All Scripture is God-breathed [given by divine inspiration] and is profitable for instruction, for conviction [of sin], for correction [of error and restoration to obedience], for training in righteousness [learning to live in conformity to God's will, both publicly and privately—behaving honorably with personal integrity and moral courage].

2 Timothy 3:16

Bringing it together:
God wants to meet every one of our needs. He wants to be the means by which we win in life. His identity gives us identity. He is a great father and he becomes all things for his children. Keep God in the loop of your life, he knows how it is supposed to unfold, get the assistance, support, directives you need to know what you need to do to ensure your life becomes all he intended it to be.

Right now, just begin to thank God for who he is.

Chapter 6

God's Approval

*And God blessed them, and God said unto them,
"Be fruitful and multiply, and replenish the earth, and
subdue it; and have dominion over the fish of the sea,
and over the fowl of the air, and over every living
thing that moveth upon the earth.*
Genesis 1:28

From the very beginning God Blessed humanity. He gave us his approval for a life well lived. Biblical blessings are given for our welfare. God is interested in your well-being as well as all of humanity.

The amplified classical version put it this way:

And God blessed them and said to them, Be fruitful, multiply, and fill the earth, and subdue it [using all its vast resources in the service of God and man]; and have dominion over the fish of the sea, the birds of the air, and over every living creature that moves upon the earth.

Genesis 1:28 (AMP)

We should be using the resources here on earth to better serve God and pushing humanity forward. Just look at the way we do life today. We are blessed because of those that used the vast resources of the earth and created things that caused us to do life on another level, efficiently and effectively.

The word Blessing comes from the Hebrew word barak meaning to invoke divine favor, to empower to be prosperous and successful. So, you don't have to try to live a blessed life. You've been empowered to live it. You have the power already given to you by God. When you empower someone you authorize, entitle, commission, certify, and qualify them.

You've been:
- Authorized
- Entitled
- Commissioned
- Certified
- Qualified

all to live a blessed life.

Below is a short list of things that the Blessing promotes:
- Anointing
- Favor
- Grace
- Health
- Wealth
- Riches
- Happiness
- Comfort
- Security/Safety
- Prosperity/Profit
- Success
- Increase
- Stewardship

Being Blessed is when God extends the advantages of being his Son or daughter to you.

Say the following out loud:
- I have an advantage over the enemy
- I have an advantage over worldly systems
- I have an advantage over anxiety, fear and worry
- I have an advantage over lack, insufficiency and poverty
- I have an advantage over infirmities, illnesses, disorders, disabilities and impairments
- I have an advantage over loneliness, limiting beliefs and social frustrations
- I HAVE AN ADVANTAGE!

Blessed shalt thou be in the city, and blessed shalt thou be in the field. Blessed shall be the fruit of thy body, and the fruit of thy ground, and the fruit of thy cattle, the increase of thy kine, and the flocks of thy sheep. Blessed shall be thy basket and thy store. Blessed shalt thou be when thou comest in, and blessed shalt thou be when thou goest out. The LORD shall cause thine enemies that rise up against thee to be smitten before thy face: they shall come out against thee one way, and flee before thee seven ways. The LORD shall command the blessing upon thee in thy storehouses, and in all that thou settest thine hand unto; and he shall bless thee in the land which the LORD thy God giveth thee. The LORD shall establish thee an holy people unto himself, as he hath sworn unto thee, if thou shalt keep the commandments of the LORD thy God, and walk in his ways. And all people of the earth shall see that thou art called by the name of the LORD; and they shall be afraid of thee. And the LORD shall make thee plenteous in goods, in the fruit of thy body, and in the fruit of thy cattle, and in the fruit of thy ground, in the land which the LORD swore unto thy fathers to give thee. The LORD shall open unto thee his good treasure, the heaven to give the rain unto thy land in his season, and to bless all the work of thine hand: and thou shalt lend unto many nations, and thou shalt not borrow. And the LORD shall make thee the head, and not the tail; and thou shalt be above only, and thou shalt not be beneath; if that thou hearken unto the commandments of the LORD thy God, which I command thee this day, to observe and to do them:

And thou shalt not go aside from any of the words which I command thee this day, to the right hand, or to the left, to go after other gods to serve them.

Deuteronomy 28:3-14

The Blessing overrides the curse, it allows you to flow in divine favor. It gives you the ability to produce. The blessing allows you to prosper in every area of your life regardless of natural circumstances. You have access to the wisdom of God and divine favor through faith that can cause you to triumph over the enemy.

You've been empowered to prosper and be successful in all arenas of life, as a:
- Parent
- Spouse
- Student
- Entrepreneur
- Employee/Professional
- Community Leader

Chapter 7

†

SUPERNATURAL APTITUDE

*But you have an anointing from the Holy One,
and you all know the truth.*
1 John 2:20

The anointing gives you the ability to do things that you normally wouldn't be able to do. The anointing is an important part of life for it is God on flesh, doing those things that the flesh cannot do, giving strategies for a quality life- a life well lived.

The Hebrew word *messiah* and the Greek word Christ both mean "the anointed one."

And it shall come to pass in that day, that his burden shall be taken away from off thy shoulder, and his yoke from off thy neck, and the yoke shall be destroyed because of the anointing.

Isaiah 10:27

The anointing gives you the power to remove burdens and destroy yokes within your sphere of influence.

A burden is anything that weighs you down so that you can't fulfil purpose. Burdens operate from the realm of limitations. You may be limited in finances, education, health, or human help and support.

A yoke in the context of this manual is a stronghold that causes us to think feel and act in ways that aren't becoming of who we were created to be. Yokes are mindsets and form habits in our lives that take us away from the promises and plans of God.

When yokes are destroyed mandates are given. A mandate is the mindset of God for our lives- brings order, direction, authorization and endorsement. Your mandate is your assignment.

The Spirit of the Lord is upon me (the Messiah), because He has anointed me to preach the Good News to the poor. He has sent me to announce release (pardon, forgiveness) to the captives and recovery of sight to the blind, to set free those who are oppressed (downtrodden, bruised, crushed by tragedy), to proclaim the favorable year of the Lord [the day when salvation and the favor of God abound greatly]." Then He rolled up the scroll [having stopped in the middle of the verse], gave it back to the attendant and sat down [to teach];

and the eyes of all those in the synagogue were [attentively] fixed on Him. He began speaking to them: "Today this Scripture has been fulfilled in your hearing and in your presence."

Luke 4:18-21 (AMP)

There is an anointing for the assignment that God has given you. It doesn't matter how small or big the assignment may seem to you. Even the smallest of things are counted big and great in the Kingdom of God. If God has instructed you to do it then he will teach, guide and instruct. You will be able to accomplish your goals, vision and purpose in this life.

Here is what the apostle Paul said: I can do all things through Christ which strengtheneth me (Philippians 4:13).

There are many anointings listed in the bible given to men and woman of those times to pursue their destiny, and all of these anointings are made available to you today. You just have to know they are there and ask for them, seek them out. The anointing is given to us to accomplish God's will and purposes- assignments. The anointings of God are good things and he withholds no good thing from those who walk with him (Psalm 84:11).

Let's look at the anointings placed on those in the Word of God walked in scripture that are made available to us today.

ANOINTINGS

SOLOMON'S ANOINTING
1 Chronicles 29
2 Chronicles 9
- Resource management
- Wisdom
- Wealth
- Success
- Prosperity

ISSAC'S ANOINTING
Genesis 26:1-14
- Investment strategies

CYRUS' ANOINTING
Ezra 1:4-11
- Financial understanding, cleverness

SAMUEL'S ANOINTING
1 Samuel 19:20
- Sensitivity and obedience to the voice of God

ESTHER'S ANOINTING
Esther 4:16
- Divine favor
- Kingdom strategies

Daniel's Anointing
Refer to entire book of Daniel
- Government
- Excellence
- Integrity

Joseph's Anointing
Psalm 105:21
- Leadership strategies
- Politics
- Business
- Economic growth

Joshua's Anointing
Joshua 6:1-3
- Warfare
- Prosperity
- Success strategies

Abraham's Anointing
Genesis 12:1-3
- Pioneering new territories
- Real-estate acquisitions
- Intergenerational covenant blessings

Moses' Anointing
Exodus. 1:22- Deuteronomy. 34:5-6
- Trailblazer
- Leadership
- Legislator

Ezra & Nehemiah's anointing
Refer to the books of Ezra & Nehemiah
- Renovator
- Restorer
- Builder
- Authentic worshipper

Deborah's anointing
Judges chapters 4&5
- Balance
- Career
- Calling
- Family

David's anointing
Book of Psalms
- Worship and praise

Paul's anointing
Refer to Romans, 1 & 2 Corinthians, Galatians, Ephesians, Philippians, Colossians
- Cutting edge apostolic revelation

Elijah's anointing
1 Kings Chapter 17 &18
- Prophetic accuracy
- Insight

Elisha's Anointing
1 Kings 19:19-21-2 Kings
- Servanthood
- Ministerial succession
- Double portion jurisdictional power and authority

Issachar's Anointing
1 Chronicles 12:32
- Discernment of correct times and seasons

Abigail's Anointing
1 Samuel 25
- Hospitality
- Prudence
- Beauty

Anna's Anointing
Luke 2:36-38
- Intercession
- Thankfulness
- Evangelistically

Christ's Anointing
Refer to Matthew, Mark, Luke, John
- Prophetic prayer
- Spiritual warfare
- Signs
- Wonders
- Miracles
- Purpose driven life

Uzziah's anointing
2 Chronicles 26:5-15
- Technological advancement

Disciple's anointing
Refer to Matthew, Mark, Luke, John
- Learning
- Trust
- Obedience
- Work ethic

Jabez's anointing
1 Chronicles 4:10
- Territorial and intellectual growth

Adam and Eve's anointing
Genesis 1:28, 30; 2:15
- Fruitfulness
- Dominion
- Responsibility
- Management

Strategies that the anointing gave rise to:
- Isaac was able to prosper during economic recession (Genesis 26:12-14).
- Jacob was able to leave a job that wasn't paying him well and became an entrepreneur and busines man (Genesis 30).
- Joseph changed the trajectory of a nation (Genesis 41).

- Gideon made use of insufficient military resources (Judges 7).
- Joshua was able to bring down the walls of Jericho (Joshua 6).
- Moses delivered his people from perverse rulership (Exodus 3-12).
- Elisha healed the water supply of a community (2 Kings 2:19-22).
- Daniel became a president (Daniel 1-2).
- A widow was able to cancel and demolish debt while creating wealth (2 Kings 4:1-7).
- Nehemiah brought about social change (Nehemiah 1-6).

Your ability to make full use of your life for the Kingdom of God is going to require you knowing your God and the anointings he has made available to you that will equip you with strategies and strength to do exploits-daring deeds (Daniel 11:32).

As you can see the anointing is given to us to effectively engage in the world and live a productive life through divine strategies. Every obstacle, stumbling block, difficulty and problem you will ever face in life will take a divine strategy to realign you with God's original intent.

Ask God for the anointing to handle challenges that arise in your life. Seek wisdom on how to activate them so that you can live the life God wants you to live-the good life.

I decree and declare that you are anointed to live successfully and victoriously in every season of your life. You are beginning to receive strategies on how to overrule, overthrow and reverse demonic activity within your life, becoming in sync with God's perfect will.

God is not a respecter of person (Acts 10:34), therefore the anointing and strategies that he gave to those of old, he can give to you as well, to keep the enemy out of a job.

Chapter 8

†

Put Your Gear On

Put on the full armor of God, so that you can take your stand against the devil's schemes. For our struggle is not against flesh and blood, but against the rulers, against the authorities, against the powers of this dark world and against the spiritual forces of evil in the heavenly realms. Therefore, put on the full armor of God, so that when the day of evil comes, you may be able to stand your ground, and after you have done everything, to stand. Stand firm then, with the belt of truth buckled around your waist, with the breastplate of righteousness in place, and with your feet fitted with the readiness that comes from the gospel of peace. In addition to all this, take up the shield of faith, with which you can extinguish all the flaming arrows of the evil one. Take the helmet of salvation and the sword of the Spirit, which is the Word of God.

Ephesians 6:11-17

Here we will discuss the wardrobe to wear to protect you against deception- schemes the enemy uses to undermine your greatness. We understand through scripture that our battle isn't a natural battle, but it is a spiritual one, so the full amour of God is spiritual gear that we need to understand if we are going to protect our spirit which is a powerful commodity- from it we get manifestations in our life, good or evil.

Armor of God

Belt of truth

The belt of truth is a winner's integrity. The belt of a solider securely holds all other pieces of clothing and armor together as well as holds weapons allowing the solider to move freely. So, truth gives two things:
- Security
- Freedom

Then Jesus turned to the Jews who had claimed to believe in him. "If you stick with this, living out what I tell you, you are my disciples for sure (security). Then you will experience for yourselves the truth, and the truth will free you (freedom).

John 8:32

Breastplate of Righteousness

The breastplate of righteousness is a winner's purity. The breastplate of a solider was used to protect his vital organs. We have need of protecting our heart (subconscious mind) to keep away from impure practices and temptations that will hinder and even stop us from releasing our greatness.

Righteousness keeps you pure, by spending time with God you filter out all self-defeating thought processes which are impure thoughts ideas and suggestions that will cause you not to live life as your authentic, true self.

Shoes of Peace

Shoes of peace is a winner's steadfastness. Soldiers would wear shoes like football cleats, to make sure they kept a grip to the ground. The enemy will throw many temptations, doubt, and discouragement to try to knock you down while you are moving toward your authentic and true self by releasing your potential and shaping history by giving back to humanity through your God given and inspired assignments. Peace allows you not to be moved.

When you are steadfast, you are:
- Loyal
- Committed
- Uncompromising
- Steady
- True
- Dependable

Shield of Faith

The shield of faith is a winner's certainty. The shields that the Roman soldiers used protected them from the arrows that soldiers in that time dipped in oil and lit up with fire. The enemy knows that a little spark he throws our way can ignite a big fire if we have unbelief. Faith extinguishes those little sparks of doubt, disappoint and temptations.

Helmet of salvation

The helmet of salvation is a winner's sanity. Helmets protected the soldiers head. Head injury could cause one to forget the truth and past experiences such as salvation. Your salvation allows you to think and behave in a normal way. When a person does not have salvation, they are insane, they have not taken on the mind of Christ, which allows us to live normal successful and prosperous lives. Normal being the way God originally intended on us to live. Salvation is the deliverance from the effects of sin. You're delivered from sin because you are raised above it and don't live your life governed by it. Your life strategies are from God- your governing factor.

Sword of the Spirit

The sword of the Spirit is the winner's offensive weapon. It is used unlike the other parts of our gear we are told to put on. The others up to this point has protected and guarded, being for our defense. Now it's time to fight back. This is what Jesus used to fight when he was tempted by Satan (Matthew 4:3-10). The Word of God is the only thing that can destroy a lie and counteract an attack.

The Word of God comes in three forms:
- Written word (Bible)
- Word made flesh (Jesus)
- Spoken Word (Holy Spirit)

Read the bible, follow Jesus, allow the Holy Spirit to work through you.

Prayer

Prayer is a part of your gear that generates power. Prayer is your place for the following:
- Forgiveness
- Realignment
- Deliverance
- Breakthrough
- Wealth creation
- Power
- Wisdom
- Healing
- Empowerment
- Comfort
- Hope
- Truth
- Peace

Prayer lays hold of God's plan and becomes the link between His will and its accomplishment on earth. Amazing things happen, and we are given the privilege of being the channels of the Holy Spirit's prayer.
- Elisabeth Elliot

We can be tired, weary, and emotionally distraught, but after spending time alone with God, we find that He injects into our bodies energy, power and strength.
- Charles Stanley

Never stop praying.

1 Thessalonians 5:17

Put on the full armor of God.

WALK IN INTEGRITY, PURITY, STEADFASTNESS, CERTAINTY, SANITY, AND GOD'S WORD.

Take all the help you can get, every weapon God has issued, so that when it's all over but the shouting you'll still be on your feet. Truth, righteousness, peace, faith, and salvation are more than words. Learn how to apply them. You'll need them throughout your life. God's Word is an indispensable weapon. In the same way, prayer is essential in this ongoing warfare. – Ephesians 6:13-18 (MSG)

When one takes on the armor of God, fear retreats into the shadows. – Brad Wilcox

Chapter 9

THE ENEMY'S PROFESSION

The thief comes to steal kill and to destroy.
John 10:10

In the world we will be tempted with many things to get us to lose our focus and forfeit our inheritance. These temptations are enemies to purpose and a fulfilled life. The enemy's job is to offer what I call carnal candies to substitute for our God given assignment, purpose and divine inheritance all in which are beneficial to our entire being.

The carnal candies I speak of will leave our life with cavities, holes in which God's glory belongs. If the enemy can get us to take a counteroffer besides God's will for our lives, he can destroy not only our life but an entire generation.

Although there are many ways to be tempted there are three categories by which the enemy in his profession of a thief uses to:
- Steal your victory
- Kill your integrity and reputation
- To destroy your legacy

These categories of Temptation are:
- The Lust of the Flesh
- The Lust of the eyes
- The Pride of Life

The Lust of the Flesh

This temptation is the temptation to feel pleasure to the body, making it satisfied. Although the body may be satisfied, it places one to be more and more separated from God spiritually. Not separated from his Love but from his Glory, the manifestation of his will in their lives. The kingdom of God cannot come forth in contaminated and perverted grounds.

Now the works of the flesh are manifest, which are these; Adultery, fornication, uncleanness, lasciviousness, idolatry, witchcraft, hatred, variance, emulations, wrath, strife, seditions, heresies, envyings, murders, drunkenness, revellings, and such like: of the which I tell you before, as I have also told you in time past, that they which do such things shall not inherit the kingdom of God."

Galatians 5:19-21

Examples of The Lust of the Flesh:
- Sexual sins
- Gossip
- Physical violence
- Drug and alcohol use

These are areas where you are physically involved in to perform. We can see in 1 Corinthians 6:19-20 that our bodies are not our own.

Do you not know that your bodies are temples of the Holy Spirit, who is in you, whom you have received from God? You are not your own; you were bought at a price. Therefore, honor God with your bodies.
1 Corinthians 6:19-20

Paul tells us in Romans 12:1 to present our bodies a living sacrifice.

We should be doing those things which are pleasing to the creator with our bodies such as:
- Marital sex (Hebrews 13:4)
- Speak to build others up (Ephesians 4:29)
- Live with others in harmony (1 Peter 3:8-9)
- Taking care of our health (3 John 1:2)

"The Spirit gives life; the flesh counts for nothing."
John 6:63

The Lust of the Eyes

In this section, I would like for us to look at the word lust before going into what the lust of the eyes is.

In very simple terminology, lust is desire gone wrong.

It is a strong and evil craving often associated with sex but as we have unfolded in the "Lust of the flesh" section, there is more to it than just sexual immorality.

God when he made humanity, he gave us the forces of thoughts, desires, feelings, imaginations, and power. He gave them to us so that we can be decision making beings, manifesting his Kingdom on earth through every choice we make. What I want to convey to you is that these things are not evil being your thoughts, desires, feelings, imaginations and power. Being human is not a disadvantage. It is not evil to desire something. In fact, the Lord will give you the desires of your heart according to Psalm 37:4.

The trick has come in because of our fallen human nature. Before the fall of man, the human nature was without flaw, we were a part of the God-class. Adam and Eve had a direct communication line to God, where they spoke to him and he spoke to them. When Adam partook of the forbitten fruit he fell from a place of control. A place where he operated in authority, responsibility and dominion because he literally had the mind of God. He fell into a place where he now became instinctive of limitations, where he forfeited the fellowship with the father because now his thoughts, desires, feelings, imaginations and power were influenced by evil.

The minds of the humans were now veiled, separating their minds from truth, reality and God's perspective.

In other words, lust is corrupted desire.

The temptation of the lust of the eyes?

It is to look upon something that is contrary to God, to your integrity, the original intent for the forces we have been given discussed previously in the above section.

The lust of the eyes has to do with the following:
- Looking upon things that God said not to
- Looking upon things without God's filter, not seeing things the way God sees them
- Looking upon things that don't belong to us, in an act of covetousness. Wanting what belongs to someone else.

Examples of lust of the eyes are:
- Pornography
- Desiring others material possessions
- Desire for Status
- Infatuated with Appearance

The Lust of the eyes is wanting things for its visual appeal, not for the sake of promoting God's Kingdom by fulfilling your assignment. It opens the door to self-promotion and self-glorifying which can lead to no real results, change or legacy.

For in him we live and move and have our being.
Acts 17:28

The eye is the lamp of the body. If your eyes are healthy, your whole body will be full of light.
Matthew 6:23

The Pride of Life

The temptation of the pride of life is when an induvial is deceived. They are deceived because they want excess power or greatness. This is deception because we are already powerful and great being made in the image and likeness of God.

Examples of Pride of Life:
- Desiring to get credit for things that others did
- Desiring to get the glory for things that God himself did
- Desiring for others to worship you
- Desiring for others to hold you in excess esteem
- Desiring to feel more important than others around you
- Desiring to have positions of power over others so that your ego is puffed, and you have "bragging rights"
- Doing things not to serve but to be served

Consider the words spoken by Lucifer (An Angel, Morning star, Bringer of Light) before becoming Satan (The adversary, opposer, accuser, tempter).
Luke 22:26

I will ascend above the heights of the clouds; I will be like the most High.

Isaiah 14:14

This very persuasion of "I will be like the most high" is what alienated him from God. It was the pride of life, wanting to be more than what he was created to be. God created him specifically to guard his presence through worship.

For by the grace [of God] given to me I say to every one of you not to think more highly of himself [and of his importance and ability] than he ought to think; but to think so as to have sound judgment, as God has apportioned to each a degree of faith [and a purpose designed for service].

Romans 12:3

Recorded accounts of temptations by Satan:

Here we will look at the first woman to be on earth as well as the life of Jesus Christ and what we will find is that they were tempted by Satan to walk contrary to God's Word.

Eve's account with temptation

And when the woman saw that the tree was good for food [lust of the flesh], and that it was pleasant to the eyes [lust of the eyes], and a tree to be desired to make one wise [the pride of life], she took of the fruit thereof, and did eat, and gave also unto her husband with her; and he did eat."

Genesis 3:6

Jesus' account with temptation

And when the tempter came to him, he said, If thou be the Son of God, command that these stones be made bread [lust of the flesh]. But he answered and said, It is written, Man shall not live by bread alone, but by every word that proceedeth out of the mouth of God.

Then the devil taketh him up into the holy city, and setteth him on a pinnacle of the temple, and saith unto him, If thou be the Son of God, cast thyself down: for it is written, He shall give his angels charge concerning thee: and in their hands they shall bear thee up, lest at any time thou dash thy foot against a stone [the pride of life]. Jesus said unto him, It is written again, Thou shalt not tempt the Lord thy God.

Again, the devil taketh him up into an exceeding high mountain, and sheweth him all the kingdoms of the world, and the glory of them [the lust of the eyes]; And saith unto him, All these things will I give thee, if thou wilt fall down and worship me. Then saith Jesus unto him, Get thee hence, Satan: for it is written, Thou shalt worship the Lord thy God, and him only shalt thou serve."

Matthew 4:3-10

Putting it into perspective:

There is nothing wrong with enjoying physical pleasure in things in which God allows us to enjoy. God created food to taste delicious so there is nothing wrong with enjoying a delicious meal, but gluttony is a sin. Sex is of God, he created it, it is a part of reproduction and becoming one flesh of the marital un-ion. We should enjoy intimacy with our spouses, adultery and fornication is sin.

There is nothing wrong with looking at beautiful things. The world is filled with beautiful buildings, structures, paintings, materials, and even creation itself is breathtaking. I, myself don't think that there is anything more beautiful than a rainbow, a mountain landscape, the ocean, or the stars. There are certain things we should avoid. When we lustfully look upon things God has commanded us to avoid, such as pornography, other people's spouses, or other people's possessions, it becomes sin.

I am an advocate of hard work and aiming for the top. There is nothing wrong with having ambition or desiring to be great! However, we must do so giving glory to God. When we desire to be praised for other's efforts, or when we desire power or knowledge for the sake of just looking good or to be seen, we become entangled in the pride of life resulting in sin.

What is sin?

The best way I can describe sin, is that it is disobedience to God that results in separation of living a divine lifestyle. Simply put, it is poor life strategies.

You must know that God has your best interest at heart and that everything he tells us to do or disallows us from doing is for our benefit. He wants us to live Blessed and Prosperous lives. Case and point, the ten commandments.

The ten commandments were instituted by God through Moses for the following reasons:
- To ensure the well-being of his people
- To govern his people's lives
- To bring an awareness to what could separate them from him
- A reminder that they need forgiveness/salvation
- To bring about a fixed purpose and structure
- To allow them to see that without him they were destined for failure and defeat

I am the LORD thy God, which have brought thee out of the land of Egypt, out of the house of bondage.

Thou shalt have no other gods before me. Thou shalt not make unto thee any graven image, or any likeness of any thing that is in heaven above, or that is in the earth beneath, or that is in the water under the earth. Thou shalt not bow down thyself to them, nor serve them: for I the LORD thy God am a jealous God, visiting the iniquity of the fathers upon the children unto the third and fourth generation of them that hate me; And shewing mercy unto thousands of them that love me, and keep my commandments. Thou shalt not take the name of the LORD thy God in vain; for the LORD will not hold him guiltless that taketh his name in vain. Remember the sabbath day, to keep it holy. Six days shalt thou labour, and do all thy work: But the seventh day is the sabbath of the LORD thy God: in it thou shalt not do any work, thou, nor thy son, nor thy daughter, thy manservant, nor thy maidservant, nor thy cattle, nor thy stranger that is within thy gates: For in six days the LORD made heaven and earth, the sea, and all that in them is, and rested the seventh day: wherefore the LORD blessed the sabbath day, and hallowed it. Honour thy father and thy mother: that thy days may be long upon the land which the LORD thy God giveth thee. Thou shalt not kill. Thou shalt not commit adultery. Thou shalt not steal. Thou shalt not bear false witness against thy neighbour. Thou shalt not covet thy neighbour's house, thou shalt not covet thy neighbour's wife, nor his man-servant, nor his maidservant, nor his ox, nor his ass, nor any thing that is thy neighbour's.

Exodus 20:1-17

The ten commandments we can view as ten life strategies. The ten commandments as we read in the book of Exodus are:
- You shall have no other gods before Me.
- You shall make no idols.
- You shall not take the name of the Lord your God in vain.
- Keep the Sabbath day holy.
- Honor your father and your mother.

- You shall not murder.
- You shall not commit adultery.
- You shall not steal.
- You shall not bear false witness against your neighbor.
- You shall not covet.

All of these are life strategies to live well and in rhythm with God.

Developing a close relationship with God and receiving the holy spirit will allow more life strategies and mysteries to be revealed to you (John 14:26, John 16:13) concerning your life and the choices you should make to get the fulfillment of your purpose.

We shouldn't even be quick to judge, because we don't know the call or plan of God for a person's life.

No eye has seen, no ear has heard, and no mind has imagined what God has prepared for those who love him.

1 Corithians2:9

If they are walking with God, then God is leading and instructing them on the decisions they should make and even if they make a wrong move, we are still instructed just to love. Here's why:

Above all keep loving one another earnestly, since love covers a multitude of sin.

1 Peter 4:8

So, if we view the ten commandments as ten life strategies, we can then view sin as missing the mark. The mark being walking in God's divine plan, his perfection by way of following his strategies.

All have missed the mark and didn't get their arrow to hit the perfection of God.

The Bible says it like this:

All have sinned and fallen short of the Glory of God.
Romans 3:23

We need Grace. Grace is the enabling power of God he gives us to fulfill his law, follow is precepts and overcome sin or poor life strategies.

By grace you have been saved through faith, and that not of yourselves; it is the gift of God, not of works, lest anyone should boast.
Ephesians 2:8-9

Moreover, the law entered, that the offence might abound. But where sin abounded, grace did much more abound.
Romans 5:20

Grace washes away all sin, no matter how small or big. There is no sin too bad or too many sins for God's grace to handle. Where sin is, grace is, much more abounding. I don't care how bad you've messed up, or how many times you've fallen into your fallen human nature. God's grace is sufficient to cover and cleanse you from all of your poor life strategies.

Three times I pleaded with the LORD to take it away from me. But he said to me, "My grace is sufficient for you, for my power is made perfect in weakness." Therefore I will boast all the more gladly about my weaknesses, so that Christ's power may rest on me.
2 Corinthians 12:8-9

God's power in you legally makes the law of sin void. It revokes its operation. Grace is an important factor in you walking in your blessed life.

Study verses of your sins being nullified.
- 1 John 1:7
- 1 John 1:9
- Romans 3:25
- Psalm 103:12
- Micah 7:19

Chapter 10

The Setup

*Be careful how you think; your life
is shaped by your thoughts.
Proverbs 4:23*

We all have picked up certain demonic thoughts, ideas and suggestions from people, places, environments and opinions associated with our schools, workplaces, families, social groups, television, social media and traditional media. Therefore, our thoughts, ideologies, suggestions and plans should come from another place. That place is the Kingdom of God, we must be in harmony with heavens frequency to live victoriously in the world because the worlds system will never work for an ambassador of the Kingdom.

If ye were of the world, the world would love his own: but because ye are not of the world, but I have chosen you out of the world, therefore the world hateth you.

John 15:19

As we discussed in the introduction it's important to use the Word of God as a filter. Filtering out all the self-sabotaging things that enter the heart of the mind.

Our mind is a great tool, its purpose is to produce our quality of life. Whether that quality of life is mundane or extraordinary.

It is God's will for you to live an extraordinary life, but you must renew your mind to experience it.

And be not conformed to this world; but be ye transformed by the renewing of your mind.

Do not be shaped by this world; instead be changed within by a new way of thinking.

Romans 12:2

This text conveys that what we experience in our lives are predicated on the thoughts in our mind. If we want a healthy, successful and prosperous life then we must first have a healthy, successful and prosperous thinking pattern and process. Nothing in your life will transform until you renew your mind.

Areas to renew your mind in are:
- Finances
- Relationships
- Marriage
- Parenting
- Business
- Health and Nutrition
- Ministry and Service
- Religion and Spirituality

ALL AREAS OF LIFE

We must live according to God's plan for each of these areas if we are going to be successful in them. We must literally get God's mind on the matter.

For my thoughts are not your thoughts, neither are your ways my ways," declares the LORD.
Isaiah 55:8

This leads me to ask the phenomenal questions that Dr. Cindy Trimm asks her audiences:

1. *Could things be the way that they are because you are the way you are?*
2. *What one thing could you change, that could change everything?*
3. *What could you change that could change the following: Financial lack, Marital Problems, Business deficiencies, Sickness and disease, Unhealthy relationships, Undiscovered Purpose or calling.*
Answer: You can always change your mind.

Set your mind on the things that are above, not on earthly things.

Colossians 3:2

Just like you would set a clock, to ensure that the time is right so that you can properly navigate through life in an organized manner, you must set your mind alike.

Setting your mind places, you in the driver's seat of your own life. You don't have to wonder were you will end up in life, you will end up, wherever you choose to end up by your thinking and corresponding actions.

As I say to my audiences on various platforms:
"Life doesn't happen to you, you happen to life."

Benefits of setting your mind:
- Purposefully navigating
- Emotionally sound
- Mentally solid
- Productive
- Healthy decisions
- Quality Lifestyle

Think on things that are true, noble, reputable, authentic, compelling, gracious- the best not the worst; the beautiful, not the ugly; things to praise, not to curse.

Philippians 4:8-9

In the above scripture Paul lists the things that we should keep our mind set on in order to be in alignment and harmonized with heaven. These things should be our governing force for our thinking for they will keep our thoughts from being moved by challenges and changed by circumstances.

Don't allow the laws of the mind to work against you. Set your mind on what you want to see materialize in your life and remain consistently, constantly the same in that thought process. This is a set up for a quality life that Jesus came to give you (John 10:10).

Chapter 11

✝

Abundant Living

You will show me the path of life; in your presence is fullness of joy; In your righthand there are pleasures forevermore.
Psalm 16:11

The creator of life knows all about life (Revelation 22:13). If the creator knows all things about life and I am a consumer of the creator's product which is life, it only makes sense to go to the creator about the functioning and operations of the product, which is life.

Many people are trying to figure this thing called life out and they are doing it without consulting with the creator. My suggestion to you is that if you want to progress in life, the best place to receive the instructions is from the creator of himself.

The creator of a product knows what it takes for that product to effectively operate releasing Joy and pleasure to its consumer.

If you be willing and obedient you will eat the good of the land.

Isaiah 1:19

I came so you can have real and eternal life, more and better life than you ever dreamed of.

John 10:10 (MSG)

Jesus came to give humanity a quality life. To restore humanity back to its original state before Adam partaken the fruit of knowledge of good and evil.

Quality of life relates to every aspect of who you are, being:
- Intellectual (Soul)
- Physical (Body)
- Spiritual (Spirit)

Quality of life is the standard of comfort, and happiness of an individual or community, engaging in a productive, fulfilling lifestyle.

There are seven components of a quality life that everyone must adhere to in order to live life abundantly.

Components of a quality life:
- Self-worth/Purpose
- Meaningful daily activities
- Belonging/Social participation

- Structure/Discipline
- Inner contentment
- Health
- Safety/Security

BREAKDOWN OF QUALITY OF LIFE COMPONENTS

In this section of the abundant life chapter, I not only break down the components of a quality life, but I ask questions to spark thinking. Don't just read the words but take time out and think to answer the questions. Your preparing for harvest devotional journal would be an excellent resource to write down your answers to the questions for continual reflection.

I. Self-worth/Purpose
- What will you not retire from?
- What could you do for free and be satisfied?
- What could you get out of bed every day to do without hesitation?
- What do you stand against?
- What do you stand for?
- What are your talents and abilities?

Self-worth is knowing your value to the world and purpose is releasing that value. We are all just clay but our purpose in life adds value to this body of clay (2nd Corinthians 4:7). It's what makes us relevant, it's our life's work.

You don't have to retire from your life's work, it's what you were born to do and when you stop doing it, it simply means it's time to go be with the father. Your life's work is accomplishments that build upon each other and you become known as an expert of it. Someone who is skilled and becomes a significant contributing member to that sector, industry, area of influence.

The opposing side of purpose is confusion. We know that God is not the author of confusion but of peace for the movement of purpose (1 Corinthians 14:33)

Success demands singleness of purpose.
– Vince Lombardi

Knowing your purpose for your life simplifies, focuses and gives meaning to your life.
– Rick Warren

II. Meaningful daily activities

- Are the things that you are involved in helping you become the person you aspire to be?
- Are you working with purpose or are you just busy?
- Does your schedule show mostly other people's agendas?
- Do your accomplishments build on each other or are they random?

Do you love life? then don't squander time, for that's the stuff that life is made of.
– Benjamin Franklin

Meaningful daily activities will lead you to the person you want to become. You can't reach goals, accomplish dreams, release potential without intentionally moving towards them daily. Being great demands great effort.

If you do what you've always done, you'll get what you've always gotten.
— Tony Robbins

You are a sum of your thoughts and actions. What you do consistently and constantly matters.

Your daily activities should include things that are beneficial to your:
- Family
- Community
- Nation
- Spiritual development
- Personal development
- Professional growth
- Goals/Ambitions/Aspirations
- Health
- Financial stability
- Security

Ask for wisdom to dominate these areas.

Teach us to number our days, that we may gain a heart of wisdom.

Psalm 90:12

Our days are numbered, we have:
- 24 hours in a day
- 168 hours in a week
- 730 hours in a month
- 8760 hours in a year

According to Genesis 6:3 God says our days on earth should be 120 years. Psalm 90:10 states 70 or 80 years, which is about what the average person lives to be today.

So, given this numeric context, let's break down how many hours one is actually looking at within their lifespan.
- 120 years = 1,051,200 hours
- 80 years = 700,800 hours
- 70 years = 613,200 hours

Given that the stages of life that we all go through such as infancy, preschool, childhood, adolescences, 18 years or 157,680 hours are really up to the adults in our life, which is why we need good responsible ones (parents, guardians, teachers, caregivers). To help us at these innocent times in our life, not to waste our life but rather help us develop- grow and become more mature, advanced, and elaborate.

David said Teach us to live wisely and well (Psalm 90:12 MSG).

Use your time wisely, you should be using your time to buy up opportunities (Colossians 4:5), don't get caught up in things that don't benefit you or the

Kingdom of God. You're going to die, you may as well die having benefitted your family, community, nation- humanity, you are a history maker. Do something great with your life. Start by allowing God to be a part of every area.

Refer back to chapter 2 and go through the ABC's of allowing the Spirit to be a part of your daily activities. **Life doesn't happen to you; you happen to life.**

In order to be successful, you must do the things today others won't do in order to have the things tomorrow that others won't have.

– Les Brown

III. Belonging/Social Participation
- What group of people do you spend most of your time with?
- Are you actively involved in your community?
- Are you apart of extracurricular activities?
- Do you go to company picnics or work parties?
- Are you a part of an auxiliary at your church?
- Do you make sure your voice is heard?

As human beings we need human interaction. God created us social beings (Genesis 2:18). Some of us need more interaction than others, but we all need some. We should be spending time and connecting with others in a positive way (Psalm 133:1). How wonderful it is to belong to a community that shares our interests and understands the why behind what we do. Life thrives from unity. When you have a sense of belonging you are happier, and you have longevity, sticking things out for the long haul.

Belonging and social participation overall increases health both physically and mentally while decreasing the risk of acquiring a disability, depression and anxiety. You cannot go through life alone and live successful and prosperous.

Belonging/Social Participation concept:
- Civic participation
- Sense of community
- Social networks and support
- Inclusiveness

Civic participation refers to individuals who are a part of their community not just in ecclesiastical spheres. Civic engagement includes communities working together in both political and non-political actions, to address public concerns and promote the quality of the community. Civic participation includes activi-ties such as volunteering, donating and voting.

Many communities have events at their local library, 5k runs and marathons and a host of nonprofit causes hold events and outreaches. Being a part of these things is considered civic participation. Find things that are going on in your community that is tied into your purpose and become a part of the evolution, if there is nothing then create something.

Benefits of civic participation:
- Greater happiness
- Social connection
- Development of skills and abilities helpful in other areas of life

Sense of community brings one to realize that they matter and are making a difference.

Benefits of sense of community:
- Healthier
- Mentally strong
- Appreciative
- Optimistic

Social networks and support are having contact with a group that helps you fulfill your purpose through providing social, emotional and financial support. These individuals are normally family and friends but are not limited to them.

Benefits of social networks and support:
- Better health
- Resources
- Emotionally sound
- Thankfulness
- Creative

Inclusiveness is when you celebrate God's diversity in ethnicities, cultures, backgrounds. It is when every individual feels valued and included. Being inclusive means to include and meet the unique needs of everyone who is functioning within that sphere.

Being inclusive is about everyone. It's about the better of the whole. Being inclusive accepts people with different backgrounds, experiences, and identities.

Benefits of being inclusive:
- Opportunities for everyone
- Positive attitudes
- Variety of Services
- Servanthood
- Community enriched programs
- Acceptance
- Unity
- Love
- Change

Without a sense of caring, there can be no sense of community.
– Anthony J. DeAngelo

Communication leads to community, that is to understand, intimacy, and mutual valuing.
– Rollo May

People coming together as a community, can make things happen.
– Jacob Reese Mobb

We don't heal in isolation but in community.
– S. Kelly Harrell

IV. Structure and discipline
- Is your home and work area organized?
- Do you have a daily routine?
- Does your day involve learning?
- Are you reaching your goals?
- Are you focused?
- Do you do what you need to do, even when you don't want to do it?

Having structure and discipline is not to limit what makes you successful and unique which is your creativity but rather makes it possible for creativity and ingenuity to flow.

It is by creating a life of structure and discipline that we learn and able to achieve greatness. Without it our life is chaotic, lacking the backbone to hold itself together causing us to be unstable and unfruitful, wasting valuable resources such as time and money.

Creating a life of structure and discipline:
Below you will be introduced to things that you can begin to implement daily to enable your creativity and ingenuity to operate uncontaminated and unhindered. You will see that you will be less stressed and more prepared as you are working on releasing your potential, pursuing success and prosperity.

Start immediately to do the following:

1. **Create a space where you can think clearly**
   This place should be:
   - Organized
   - Inspirational
   - Clean
   - Relaxing

"Thinking spaces" help you to feel yourself and get into a flow of creativity and positivity allowing you to get lost in your assignment, your work.

2. **Plan your week**
   Typically, at the beginning of the week such as Sunday. You should have a planner and calendar.
   - Prepared
   - Organized
   - Able to handle obstacles

3. **Form a checklist**
   This should be well ordered with high priorities being first.
   - Management of time and money

4. **Write things down (refer to Preparing for Harvest journal)**
   - It clears your mind for higher-level thinking
   - It helps you process your emotions
   - It makes you more committed

4. **Read**

Reading is to the mind what exercise is to the body
- Increases vocabulary
- Enhances problem solving
- Improves memory
- Reduces stress

5. **Drink water**
- Improves energy level
- Improves brain function
- Clears toxins
- Promotes breathing

6. **Get sleep**
- Improves productivity
- Enhances concentration
- Regulates immune system
- Makes you sociable

7. **Limit Social Media/ Television**

High amounts of "screen time" is associated with:
- Obesity
- Sleep problems
- Poor work and school performance
- Unhealthy risky behaviors

V. Inner contentment
- Do you consider yourself an anxious person?
- Do the things around you determine your mood?
- Are you thankful for what you have?
- Do you lose focus of your goals quickly?

External stimuli must be managed to go through life with thanksgiving (Psalms 100:4), moving toward your bright future with Joy. What this means is that you must monitor what comes through your gates (Proverbs 4:23). Because what comes through them has direct passageway to your heart, the heart of the mind. This is your subconscious.

Your gates are your Eyes, Ears, and Mouth.

In an evil prevalent society, we are constantly bombarded with opportunities to be hopeless (John 16:33). Therefore, we must continue in the Word of God, to be unmoved (1 Corinthians 15:58).

The Word of God should fill our gates. Our eyes, ears and mouth. Serving as a preventive of hopelessness and aiding in inner contentment.

Becoming a gatekeeper:

Gatekeepers were mentioned often in scripture, they were influential in maintaining order in the societies. They were guards for protection, having to be trustworthy and alert to things that could put civilization in harm. We can pull out the natural responsibility of gatekeepers and apply the principals into our spiritual life of gatekeeping.

Principals of gatekeeping:
- Maintain order
- Protect
- Trustworthy
- Alertness

Creating an atmosphere of gatekeeping:

You can implement methods of operations I call them the core 8, into your life that creates an ambience that allows you to have inner contentment, you can get through anything with these methods (Philippians 4:12-13).

Being a gate keeper is essential to releasing your potential. These core 8 are key to success at inner contentment.

Methods of operation: (Core 8)
- Faith (1 John 5:4)
- Vision/focus (Proverbs 29:18)
- Prayer (Philippians 4:6), (1 Thessalonians 5:17)
- Meditation (Isaiah 26:3) (Psalm 49:3)
- Thinking (Colossians 3:2)
- Worship and fasting (Acts 13:2)
- Learning/ Developing (Titus 3:14)
- Working (Proverbs 12:11)

With inner contentment you can move forward in life, not being stagnated which leads to the lack of growth. God is a God of growth (Deuteronomy 1:11) (1 Corinthians 3:7) Be content with where you are as you pursue where you are going. The Core 8 focuses you on where you are going and not on what's currently happening and teaches you how to be thankful. Don't be seduced out of your place of power and dominion by allowing the demonic force of discontent to come into your spirit.

So, we fix our eyes not on what is seen, but on what is unseen, since what is seen is temporary, but what is unseen is eternal.

2nd Corinthians 4:18

VI. Health
- Do you have enough energy to complete your assignment for that day?
- Do you eat meals that give you the nutrients you need?
- Do you keep your emotions in check? How?
- Are you in alignment with the higher power?
- Are you integral?
- What does your social life look like?

Your health is important as a matter of fact it is the most important part of you that God cares about (3 John 1:2). It is the state of being in good condition, the quality of being competent and reliable, undivided making one whole being brought into perfect harmony with God.

Health is a call from God, it is his will for each individual to live a healthy lifestyle, consecrated and set apart (1 Peter 1:16).

The constituents of being a healthy individual:

Health is multifaceted and consist of being:
- Physically fit
- Nutritionally well
- Emotionally sound
- Spiritually congruent
- Socially moral
- Professionally ethical
- Mentally resilient
- Financially adept

The above are the constituents or ingredients to have a healthy lifestyle. We all should be working towards excellence in them all. This doesn't happen overnight but consciously being aware of our choices and decisions we make regarding each aspect.

God loved you enough to send his son to give you an abundant life (John 10:10), it was his way of satisfying his love that he had for you (Ephesians 2:4). You should love yourself enough to live a healthy lifestyle (Ephesians 5:29). Life is not about just acquiring more but becoming more. Health is the avenue to becoming that more.

The purpose of our journey is to restore ourselves to wholeness.
– Debbie Ford

As you are restored to wholeness you will begin to live out God's original intent for your life.

VII. Safety/Security
- Do you feel safe at home?
- Do you feel safe at work?
- Do you feel safe at school?
- Do you feel safe financially?
- What are somethings apart of your life that put you in harm's way?
- What can you do to increase your safety and security?
- Are your concerns about safety and security external or internal?

In this world we have concerns about safety and security in many areas of our lives causing anxiety. We weren't built to handle high dosages of anxiety that many people face in today's time causing countless amounts of illnesses and premature deaths.

Do not be anxious about anything, but in every situation, by prayer and petition, with thanksgiving, present your requests to God.

Philippians 4:6

> Cast all your anxiety on him because he cares for you.
>
> *1 Peter 5:7*

Safety and security concerns:
- Nationally
- Financially
- Workplace
- Domestically
- Physically
- Emotionally
- Environmentally
- Spiritually

It is a promise of God to give you safety and security. Don't be deceived into thinking that safety and security come from the things of the world such as: Money, comforts, position, power. Those things can change and will change sooner or later. We must put our trust in something that will never change (Hebrews 13:18), in whom is everlasting.

> I lift up my eyes to the mountains—
>   where does my help come from?
> My help comes from the LORD,
>   the Maker of heaven and earth.
> He will not let your foot slip—
>   he who watches over you will not slumber;
> indeed, he who watches over Israel
>   will neither slumber nor sleep.

The LORD watches over you—
>   the LORD is your shade at your right hand;
> the sun will not harm you by day,
>   nor the moon by night.
> The LORD will keep you from all harm—
>   he will watch over your life;
> the LORD will watch over your coming and going
>   both now and forevermore.

Psalm 121:1

Therefore, you shall do my statutes and keep my rules and perform them, and then you will dwell in the land securely. The land will yield its fruit, and you will eat your fill and dwell in it securely.

Leviticus 25:18-19

But when you go over the Jordan and live in the land that the LORD your God is giving you to inherit, and when he gives you rest from all your enemies around, so that you live in safety

Deuteronomy 12:10

It is important to walk with God while you're on earth and be where he wants you to be, this provides protection (2 Corinthians 3:17). Spiritually by accepting Jesus as your Lord and savior you are seated in heavenly places (Ephesians 2:6), escaping eternal damnation.

Nothing can bring a real sense of Security except love.
                              -Billy Graham

And so, we know and rely on the love God has for us. God is love. Whoever lives in love lives in God, and God in them.

John 4:16

Quality of life chart:

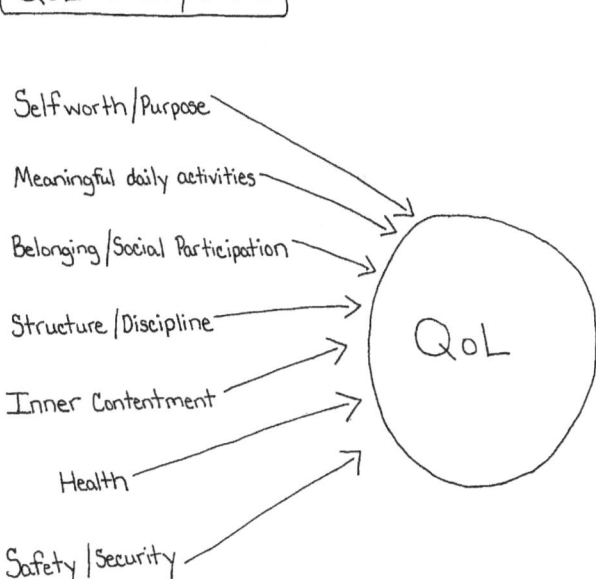

The quality, not the longevity, of one's life is what is important.

– Martin Luther King

God is very interested in your wellbeing; he wants you happy. I have included a formula for happiness that puts you in charge of it and not anyone or anything.

Formula for happiness chart:

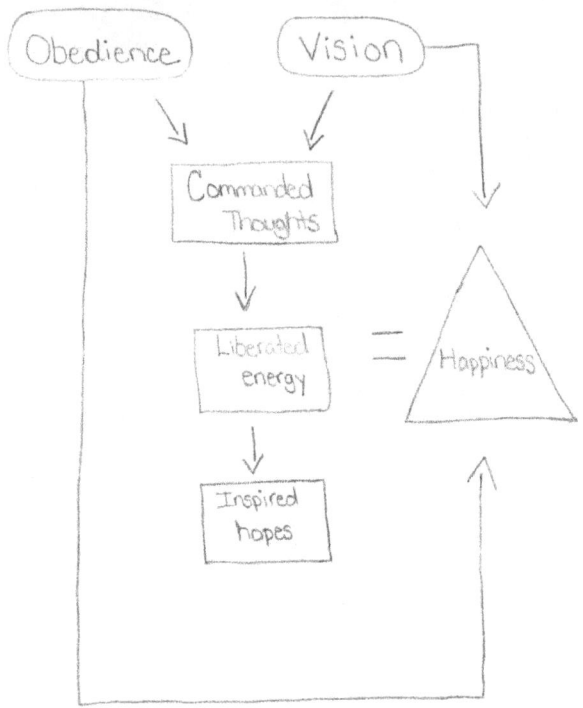

Obedience is listening & applying Gods instructions.
Vision is the mental picture, idea of your life in the future.

Happiness is not a goal; it is a by-product.
— Eleanor Roosevelt

- Have a vision that command your thoughts
- Have a vision that liberates your energy
- Have a vision that inspire your hopes

Where there is no vision, the people perish: but he that keepeth the law of God (Obedience), happy is he.
Proverbs 29:18

Chapter 12

Say so for Yourself

Commit to turning to this section of this manual daily and just read off each power packed point. You can do this as many times throughout your day as you deem necessary for inspiration, encouragement, edification, to stir your thoughts back into position for a thriving life.

When you wake up in the morning, during lunch break, before retiring for the night or during any leisure time that you'll have would be the ideal times to reflect on these pints. It will release a freshness, a dose of inspiration, and a shot of motivation to carry on in the race (Matthew 24:13).

These power packed points will feed your faith and starve out all your doubts. Power packed points produce power packed people.

I decree and declare:
- That you will begin to conduct your affairs accordingly
- That your mindset will change to place you in a place of automatic success and prosperity
- Each point that you read will cause you to experience the abundant life Jesus came that you may experience

Power Packed Points

- My words unlock my destiny
- Earth obeys a God image
- Satan wants me to talk contrary to the Word of God
- The believer's language is faith
- After being born again I must learn how to live by faith
- The devil loves confusion, I must have a fixed purpose
- The will of God is not automatic
- Godly emotions are designed to take me to purpose
- Satan attacks the soul
- My spirit is victorious if I'm born again

- Confess the invisible, believe the impossible
- There is a difference between non-existent and not a manifestation
- I can't practice small and play big
- God gives vision, I create the plan, God critiques the plan
- God will not give direction if I am not thinking.
- Man thinks and God directs
- I will be as successful as I think
- God will always take me forward, not backwards
- If God desires to lead me, then I must be willing to follow
- God's vision and perception is perfect
- Godly thoughts produce encouragement, confidence and peace
- Faith is a spiritual force, effecting natural change
- A born-again spirit is as alive to God as it will ever be
- Worship is displayed in my daily activities
- My assignment is on earth, not heaven
- I have the integrity and character of God
- God's Word should always have final authority
- God's vision and perception is perfect
- Love must be my motivation for my desires and dreams
- I must trust God even when I cannot trace him

- The enemy can only attack me in my soul
- My spirit has the victory, I follow the spirit for a victorious life
- I must understand what I have in Christ
- Faith is not taking a chance but knowing what is already made available in the heavenlies
- Faith is important but I still must work Godly principals for my faith not to be dead
- From one level of glory to another, is a process
- The way I conduct my affairs is important because we represent the Kingdom of God
- Cares are distractions from God's perfect will for my life
- Prayer is a way of life, by it I grow and overcome
- Thanksgiving is every day for Jesus has won my victory even if I don't see it naturally
- Flesh is flesh and spirit is spirit
- I live in one world but operate from the laws and principals of another
- Anointing carries more power than titles
- There will be warfare, but I must still work my vision
- For every problem, God has a prescription
- I have power to create
- I must learn spiritual warfare
- Let the misery that has challenged my life pass

- Jesus is the answer to my earthly problems not just my solution for heaven
- It's not what people say about me that maters but what God has decreed
- A resting soul produces a resting life
- Be whole enough to minister to other people's needs
- Life can be better than a fairy tale
- I must push forward with understanding
- Unmasking myself is true worship
- My value does not come because I love God but because he loves me
- Renewing my mind is a Daily exercise
- Vision causes me to escape stagnation
- Being humble causes me to escape destruction
- I am inconsistent without God
- Destiny will cost me everything
- Difficult situations produce strength, revealing to me who I am
- Responsibility is favor from God
- What I worship, I serve
- God wants to set me free and keep me free
- I am complete in Christ
- I never let emotions lead me
- Faith is equal opportunity
- Faith is an action, not just a fact

- When I know who I am, the enemy releases me
- I am the image of God, CELEBRATE!
- Souls develop in church
- I live to prove God is good, not that I am good
- I am called to sanctification
- I must sow the seed of God's Word into people's lives
- God gives me security and assurance
- Confusion stops movement, HANDLE THE CONFUSION
- A well-developed mind is equivalent to a well lived life
- Focus is how I get the promises of God
- Love people but deny access to places that God should be filled in
- I am intelligent, able to think, decide and make choices
- I place life in good hands, God himself
- I should have mutually beneficial relationships
- Jesus took failure and defeat to the cross
- I am to contribute to my family, church, community, and nation
- Grace is made available for me to run my race
- Greatness takes sacrifices
- Life is made of time, I use my time wisely
- The earth is my inheritance

- Good stewardship results in released inheritance
- My life should have the "wow factor"
- Being separate from God isn't an option for my success
- I should have a luxurious lifestyle supplied by God not credit
- With the Holy Spirit in me, I become unstoppable, able to achieve
- Read more, write more, talk more, learn more, study more, travel more
- Think, learn succeed
- Persist until success happens
- Don't be afraid of men and their faces, Go Boldly
- I prepare for what I've been praying for
- Sleep well, eat good, laugh often and work smart
- Know that the Word of God is my weapon against the enemy or enemies
- I am healthy
- I am wealthy
- I am wise
- I am happy
- I am cheerful
- I am strong
- I am powerful
- I am tenacious
- I am rich

- I am abundant
- I am bountiful
- I am lively
- I am energetic
- I am honorable
- I am courage's
- I am educated
- I business savvy
- I am finically prosperous
- I am physically thriving
- I am charitable
- I am a piece of the creator
- I am wonderful
- I am impressive
- I am whole
- I am set apart
- I am a master
- I am an over achiever
- I am a go getter
- I am walking brilliance
- I am a pleasure to be around
- I am wise council
- I am overjoyed
- I am successful
- I am fortunate
- I am honest

- I am integral
- I am daring
- I am prudent
- I am discerning
- I am opulent
- I am connected to the source
- I am charming
- I am understanding
- I am influential
- I am complete
- I am strategic
- I am immeasurable
- I am breathtaking
- I am a peacemaker
- I am generous
- I am boundless
- I am a great speaker
- I am an excellent communicator
- I am cutting edge
- I am a trailblazer
- I am saved
- I am delivered
- I am outstanding
- I am enough
- I am creating the life of my dreams
- I belong on earth

- I'm bigger than the challenges I face
- I am flexible to change
- I am unique, I'm me, the only one just like me
- I go the extra mile
- I take responsibility for my life
- Strength and courage flows through me
- I smile without reason
- I receive love and respect
- I give love and respect
- I live a balanced life
- I make improvements when and where needed
- I keep going against all odds
- I was created perfectly, and trials and tribulation keep me perfected
- I submit to God's will for my life
- God hears my prayers and delivers me out of all my troubles
- I align my prayers with God's plan and purpose
- I am not anxious about life, for I live by faith
- I keep my mind on God and he keeps me in perfect peace
- God's hands are welcoming
- God send me all the right people to work with and for me, for the fulfillment of his purposes
- I receive God's grace
- I am in faith and the Holy Spirit is in me

- God never sleeps nor slumbers therefore he is always available to me
- I forgive others and God forgives me
- I am exalted because I am humble
- I make prayerful decisions
- I am a purpose driven individual
- I am guided into truth
- Heaven is not depleted by my request
- I breathe in the breath of life daily
- God takes pleasure in my prosperity
- God wants me to have good success
- God is concerned about my soul, mind, will, emotions
- I am concerned about other people's mind, will, emotions, therefore I am careful how I treat people and engage in my affairs
- God is my healer
- God is my peace
- God is my provider
- I will rejoice always
- I will pray continually
- I will give thanks in all circumstances
- God is worthy of all my praises
- God restores my soul
- God loves me unconditionally

If you are going to see the manifestation of God's will in your life than you must begin to leave the clutter of the common- the sphere of familiarity, comfort and mediocrity where most people spend their lives. You have to begin to implement the concepts and principals to see change. You cannot only be a hearer, speaker or reader of the Word you must be a doer as well (James 1:22). Take ownership of your life, you are responsible for becoming the person God intended you to be-GREAT! Do something with your life! Life doesn't happen to you; you happen to life.

It's your season to make things happen!

An ounce of practice is worth more than tons of preaching.
– Mahatma Gandhi

The price of greatness is responsibility.

– Winston Churchill

CLOSING PRAYER

Father and my God I take you for your word. I acknowledge what Jesus did on the cross for me. He made me a son and allowed me to be seated in heavenly places in Christ. You hold no good thing from those that walk uprightly, so I make the decision to commit my ways to you. Victories are won in the spirit realm before the disclosure hits earth, so father I decree and declare victory in my life: my family, finances, workplace, church, ministry and body. I confess that the fruit of the Spirit characterize my life, I am working in perfect harmony with your plan so that your purposes will prevail in the earth, causing me to take new territory: spiritually, emotionally, relationally and professionally. I am blessed, empowered to prosper, daily loaded with benefits that is progressing me forward, breaking me out of satanic bondage that's keeping me from operating with: honesty, integrity, morality, holiness, purity, reliability. By remaining in your Word, I will be totally transformed.

I decree **MY SEASON IS HERE!**
In the name of Jesus, **SO BE IT!**

Glossary

All definitions are from the context of the Kingdom for you to have a more enlightened understanding and for easier application of scripture and the resources of "Preparing for Harvest" and "It's Your Season"

Anointing- The means by which an individual can overcome obstacles and limitations in an area or areas. It is the burden removing and yoke destroying power of God.

Assignment- Work given to an individual to complete that builds onto purpose. Assignments make up purpose, they are small contributions to the bigger plans and purposes of God.

Attitude- A frame of mind that gives the perspective on how you think, feel and believe about the world. It is your viewpoint, working for you or against you.

Blessing- An empowerment to succeed and prosper, to be commissioned to do great things in excellence.

Character- Mental and moral attributes that define who an individual is, being godly or corrupted.

Community- A group of people who share values, interest, attitudes and goals. A community gathers strength from each other making it a unit of force.

Destiny- The result of a person's thoughts, words and actions. To get God's destiny for a life an individual must think, say and do as God has purposed them to.

Discipline- The training needed to regulate a person's life so that they can live beyond temptations, emotions, self-defeating thoughts and limiting conditions. It is the conditioning for fulfilling purpose and maximizing potential.

Freedom- Being brought into the knowledge of who you are, so that you can live authentically, not conforming to corrupted systems and patterns of this world. Being free from ignorance.

Fruit- The manifestation of your attitude, character and discipline.

Happiness- Ones overall satisfaction with life, achieving those things in which they set out to achieve instructed by God.

Harvest- The return on your investment of applying principals and precepts.

Health- The state of being whole.

Humanity- Those created in the image and likeness of God, human beings collectively.

Influence- The ability to have an impact on a person through your expertise and leadership, being able to guide their behavior and development without coercion.

Joy- The strength in knowing who's you are, to push through hardship.

Kingdom- A place ruled by a King, the Kingdom of God is within us, making us governed by God the King himself.

Learning- The possession of knowledge by experiences, studying and being taught by God and those who he places in areas of influence.

Life- The very Glory of God himself.

Longevity- Being in service for a substantial amount of time, being able to add value while remaining in a learning juncture.

Mediocrity- Living beneath your privileges.

Mediation- A mental and spiritual practice to become aware, clear and calm. To extend focus on a thing so that you become it and experience it.

Prayer- Communicating with God. Talking to him and he talking to you. Having devotion.

Preparing- To align something or someone up for the expected end.

Prosperity- Having enough resources to pursue purpose and enough to overcome obstacles and give to help others in need. To live in a place of overflow.

Potential- Ones dormant ability, reserved power, untapped strength, unused success, hidden talents, and capability.

Purpose- The reason behind why something or someone was created and exist. Purpose is the gateway that leads to success.

Quality- The level of excellence that someone lives by or something is characterized by being compared to others in its specialty.

Self-worth– Honoring the God in self, assurance that one can handle their assignments.

Sin- Poor judgments, wrong strategies for getting through life and experiencing God's goodness.

Skill- To become disciplined in an area where one can become an expert.

Success- Fulling one's purpose.

Thankful- To appreciate all that life in tells, the good and not so good, taking confidence in knowing that all things work together for the fulfilling of your purpose.

Thought process- The course of action of using the mind to use knowledge gained to come up with a careful, considerate decision

Values- The principals and precepts of God about what life is all about.

ABOUT THE AUTHOR

JERRY WALKER is an Ambassador for the Kingdom of God, Author, teacher and empowerment speaker. He delivers the Word of God with authority, effectiveness, clarity and eloquence. Ambassador Walker shares with his audience that they are fearfully and wonderfully made, without defect only inaccurate thought processes.

Walker is a thought leader ushering in God's presence for the next generation, giving them Kingdom context for a life well-lived. His ministry goes beyond the church building, into the education system, political system and medical system to name a few.

Walker continues his ministry at home as he serves his wife and their three children, fulfilling 1 Corinthians 13:4-7.

To book Ambassador Walker:
Email bookambassadorwalker@gmail.com
Stay connected!
Follow on Social Media:
YouTube @ Ambassador Jerry Lee Walker III
Facebook @ Jerry Lee Walker III
Instagram @ IamJerryWalkeriii

J. Kenkade
PUBLISHING®

Our Motto
"Transforming Life Stories"

Self-Publish Your Book With Us

Our All-Inclusive Self-Publishing Package

Professional Proofreading & Editing
Interior Design & Cover Design
Manuscript Writing Assistance
Ghostwriting & More

For Manuscript Submission or other inquiries:
www.jkenkadepublishing.com
(501) 482-JKEN

Also Available from this Author

ISBN: 978-1-944486-19-8
Purchase at www.jkenkadepublishing.com

Life shouldn't be happening to us: we should be happening to life. This is what living in excellence is all about: Using every talent, gift, capacity and revelation that God has equipped us with and reaching our fullest potential. In this 31-Day guide, you will discover how meditating and reflecting on the word of God can pull you into His divine plan for your life. Prepare to expand past mediocrity and live a life of excellence.

Also Available from J. Kenkade Publishing

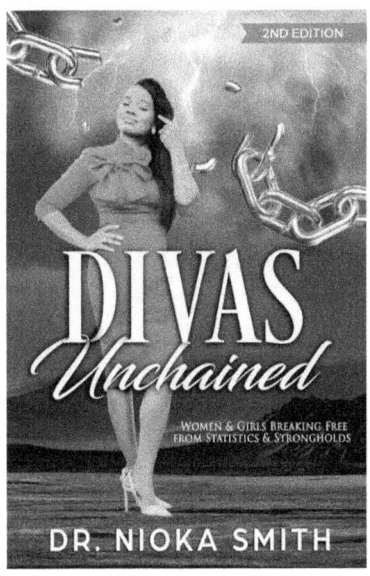

ISBN: 978-1-944486-25-9
Visit www.drniokasmith.com
Author: Dr. Nioka Smith

Sexually abused by her father at the age of 14, pregnant at the age of 17, and a nervous breakdown at the age of 28, Dr. Nioka Smith's painful past almost killed her, until the voice of the Lord guided her into destroying strongholds and reversing Satan's plan for her life. DIVAS Unchained is the powerful chain-breaking reality of the many unfortunate strongholds our women and girls face. Dr. Nioka uses her divine gift to help women and girls break free from destructive life cycles and prosper in all areas of life. Satan has lied to you. It's time to expose his lies. It's time to break free!

Also Available from J. Kenkade Publishing

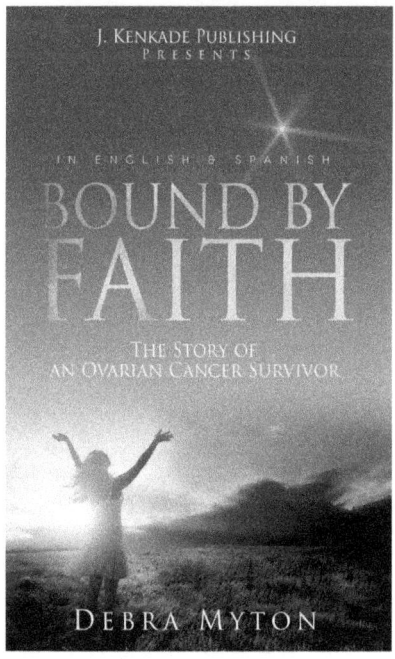

ISBN: 978-1-944486-20-4
Purchase at www.jkenkadepublishing.com

As a school counselor and mother, the author became extremely concerned about her ovarian cancer diagnosis, nutrition, and weight loss. Research shows that people do not get second opinions about their health, although health professionals do not see second opinions as a breach of trust from people. This book is a personal guide on how to handle any illness that a man or woman may face in life. This personal cancer story will make you laugh, cry, but overall, will empower you by faith. Join Debra in her journey of survival in "Bound by Faith".

Also Available from J. Kenkade Publishing

ISBN: 978-1-944486-39-6
Visit www.jkenkadepublishing.com
Author: Ramona Freeman

"Prayer: My Incense to God" is a composition of prayers created by the author over the years for various topics. The purpose of this prayer manual is to set a foundation of prayer and intercession according to the Word of God, to establish prayer in every home, city, state, and nation, and to pray the will of God in order to see His kingdom come on Earth as it is in Heaven (Matthew 6:10).

This page intentionally left blank by J. Kenkade Publishing

www.ingramcontent.com/pod-product-compliance
Lightning Source LLC
Chambersburg PA
CBHW031349040426
42444CB00005B/241